ACKNOWLEDGMENTS AND FOREWORD

First of all, I would like to take this opportunity to thank all of those who supported and motivated me during the production of this book.

Special thanks go to my girlfriend. She motivated me throughout the work and did not mind that I put so much of our free time into this project - thank you, honey!

I would also like to thank Elias D. who helped me to keep the wording as clear and understandable as possible. And he also corrected some of my spelling mistakes.

WHAT TO EXPECT FROM THAT BOOK

What you can expect in this book is above all an introduction to programming with assembly as well as an insight into the approach to various solutions for common tasks using some practical examples.

If you expect a closer look at various CPU architectures and page-long discussions about the internal processes of the CPU, I would like to recommend the Intel developer manual, which is over 4,000 pages thick. We want to take a more practical approach here and focus primarily on the basic understanding of assembly and the challenges of this particular type of programming.

Of course, I will briefly outline the most important basics and then go into more detail in practical tasks to further deepen the basic knowledge.

MARK B.

64-bit assembly programming for Linux

The easy guide to get started

IMPRINT

ISBN:

979-8555204431

Printed and bound by KDP - Kindle Direct Publishing
Published by Sharanych Media[SM]
160 00 Praha 6, Czech Republic

INDEX

ASSEMBLY LANGUAGE AND OPCODES

The following two notations can be distinguished based on the syntax:

AT&T syntax:
```
mov     $0x1, %rax
```

and

Intel-Syntax:
```
mov     rax, 0x1
```

As you can see, the arguments are reversed at AT&T and the Intel syntax, further the Intel syntax is somewhat reduced. We will only use Intel syntax in this book.

Assembly as a language uses the instruction set of the CPU. This allows, for example, programs to be perfectly optimized for the corresponding hardware. On the other hand, programs are not portable in this way, since one uses, for example, `syscalls` of the operating system and possibly special command sets of a certain CPU family or generation.

So you can get the maximum performance of the hardware, but in extreme cases, this would also mean that a program would not be able to run on another PC with the same operating system but a different CPU. The same naturally applies to a PC with identical hardware but a different operating system.

A CPU only understands binary inputs - a sequence of ones and zeros. The `mov rax, 0x1` command shown above would look like this in binary:

```
10111000000000001000000000000000000000000000000
```

Since this long column of numbers is somewhat unwieldy, the hexadecimal notation is usually used to represent opcodes (operation codes) - e.g. b801000000. Usually, these are split up again into individual bytes for better readability: b8 01 00 00 00

So opcodes are nothing more than machine commands. Since most people could not work well with b801000000 or with the binary representation of it, assembly languages have been developed. These are also called 2nd generation programming languages. Using instead of binary code abbreviations from English are easier to read - the so-called mnemonics such as `mov` for move, `sub` for subtract, `mul` for multiply, ...

The assembler as a program for creating executable files does a lot more than just convert mnemonics into opcodes. The program also relieves us of some of the work in development, for example by making macros available and / or converting them and doing various calculations for us.

Let's look at the executable file of the "Hello World" example in a hex editor:

```
00000000: 7f 45 4c 46 02 01 01 00 00 00 00 00 00 00 00 00  .ELF............
00000010: 02 00 3e 00 01 00 00 00 cd 00 40 00 00 00 00 00  ..>.......@.....
00000020: 40 00 00 00 00 00 00 00 70 02 00 00 00 00 00 00  @.......p.......
00000030: 00 00 00 00 40 00 38 00 02 00 40 00 06 00 05 00  ....@.8...@.....
00000040: 01 00 00 00 05 00 00 00 00 00 00 00 00 00 00 00  ................
00000050: 00 00 40 00 00 00 00 00 00 00 40 00 00 00 00 00  ..@.......@.....
00000060: db 00 00 00 00 00 00 00 db 00 00 00 00 00 00 00  ................
00000070: 00 00 20 00 00 00 00 00 01 00 00 00 06 00 00 00  .. .............
00000080: dc 00 00 00 00 00 00 00 dc 00 60 00 00 00 00 00  ..........`.....
00000090: dc 00 60 00 00 00 00 00 0d 00 00 00 00 00 00 00  ..`.............
000000a0: 0d 00 00 00 00 00 00 00 00 00 20 00 00 00 00 00  ..........  .....
000000b0: b8 01 00 00 00 bf 01 00 00 00 48 be dc 00 60 00  ..........H...`.
000000c0: 00 00 00 00 ba 0d 00 00 00 0f 05 eb 02 eb e1 b8  ................
000000d0: 3c 00 00 00 bf 00 00 00 00 0f 05 00 48 65 6c 6c  <...........Hell
000000e0: 6f 20 57 6f 72 6c 64 21 0a 00 00 00 00 00 00 00  o World!........
000000f0: 00 00 00 00 00 00 00 00 00 00 00 00 00 00 00 00  ................
          ... output shortened
```

For example, we recognize our opcode b8 01 00 00 00 for mov rax, 0x1 and we also see the text "Hello World!". Let's take a step forward here and I'll show you the line that defines the text:

```
text db "Hello World!", 0xA
```

Here, text is a so-called label that we can use to address the storage address of the text. db stands for define byte and the final 0xA is nothing more than the hexadecimal notation for the newline character.

The opcode 48 be dc 00 60 00 00 00 00 00 stands for movabs rsi, 0x6000DC which we use to inform the program that the text starts at the address 0x6000DC. The assembler calculates these for us and replaces every occurrence of text in the program with that memory address.

As we will see later in the program the command mov rsi, which we wrote in the source gets converted to movabs which is used to load a 64-bit address into a register. So not only the memory addresses calculated and set correctly, but also the code gets tweaked and optimized.

We want to use SASM as the IDE for assembly. SASM is available for Linux and Windows and can be downloaded from `https://dman95.github.io/SASM/english.html`. The IDE can handle MASM, FASM, NASM and GAS code. The IDE also offers a debugger, which we will use more often later.

Please download the corresponding installation file, install, and start the program. If you click on `Settings -> Settings` and open the `create`-tab in that dialogue, please fill in the appropriate lines and fields as follows:

SASM Einstellungen

Allgemein	Farben	Erstellen

Modus: ◯ x86 ⦿ x64

Assembler: ⦿ NASM ◯ GAS ◯ FASM ◯ MASM

Assembler Einstellungen:
```
-g -f elf64 $SOURCE$ -l $LSTOUTPUT$ -o $PROGRAM.OBJ$
```

Linker Einstellungen:
```
$PROGRAM.OBJ$ -o $PROGRAM$
```

Assembler Pfad:
```
nasm
```

Linker Pfad:
```
ld
```

Objektdatei Name:
```
program.o
```

Build in current directory: ▣

Linken ausschalten: ☐

NUMBER SYSTEMS

If we work with assembly, we should also take a brief look at the most important number systems.

In the case of such a long column of zeros and ones or a character string like `b801000000` it may be relatively clear which number system it is, but numbers such as `10` or `100` can be binary, decimal and hexadecimal notation. Therefore, binary numbers are prefixed with `0b` and hexadecimal numbers with `0x` to explicitly indicate the number system used. Alternatively, you can add `b` or `h` at the rear to mark a value as binary or hexadecimal.

The following five commands are synonymous:

```
mov rax, 0b1010
mov rax, 1010b
mov rax, 0xA
mov rax, 0Ah
mov rax, 10
```

In each of the cases, the decimal number `10` is assigned to the register `rax`. We'll take a look at what exactly registers are in one of the following chapters. In this example, you would have to make sure that you write `0Ah`, not just `Ah`, otherwise the assembler would assign the value from the `ah` register. With clear numbers such as `10h` for the decimal value `16`, a leading `0` is not necessary.

I prefer the spelling with `0b10` or `0x10` because in this case, such an error could not happen at all!

The hexadecimal number system
... is based on 16. Here the numbers 0-9 stand for the respective values, A corresponds to 10, B corresponds to 11, etc. up to the letter F which stands for 15.

The binary number system
... is based on 2. So only the digits `0` and `1` are used to represent a number.

Let's take a look at a few examples:

	binary	hexadecimal	decimal
10	0x1 + 1x2 = 2	0x1 + 1x16 = 16	0x1 + 1x10 = 10
11	1x1 + 1x2 = 3	1x1 + 1x16 = 17	1x1 + 1x10 = 11
100	0x1 + 0x2 + 1x(2x2) = 4	0x1 + 0x16 + 1x(16x16) = 256	0x1 + 0x10 + 1x(10x10) = 100
110	0x1 + 1x2 + 1x(2x2) = 6	0x1 + 1x16 + 1x(16x16) = 272	0x1 + 1x10 + 1x(10x10) = 110
111	1x1 + 1x2 + 1x(2x2) = 7	1x1 + 1x16 + 1x(16x16) = 273	1x1 + 1x10 + 1x(10x10) = 111

If this was going too fast for you or if you don't feel like doing those calculations, then I can only recommend you to use a calculator program or the Python Shell:

```
>>> bin(0xb801000000)
'0b1011100000000000100000000000000000000000'

>>> hex(0b1011100000000000100000000000000000000000)
'0xb801000000'

>>> int('0xb801000000', 16)
790290759680

>>> int('0b1011100000000000100000000000000000000000', 2)
790290759680

>>> hex(790290759680)
'0xb801000000'

>>> bin(790290759680)
'0b1011100000000000100000000000000000000000'
```

For the sake of completeness, I should also mention the octal number system, which is based on 8 and only uses the digits 0-7.

If you would like to know how to calculate in the different number systems and / or how to manually converted between you will find various math tutorials on Youtube.

THE AGONY OF CHOICE

As I have already indicated, there is not just one assembler and we can choose between different assemblers. There are, for example, MASM from Microsoft, FASM, NASM, GAS, etc.

The basic commands are the same between the different assemblers, but in detail, there are many differences in the specific macros, abbreviations and commands that the assembler provides itself.

To look at this, let's compare two "Hello World" examples in FASM and NASM:

FASM

```
format ELF64 executable 3

segment readable executable
    entry _start
    _start:
        mov     rax, 1
        mov     rdi, 1
        lea     rsi, [msg]
        mov     rdx, 13
        syscall

        mov     rdi, 0
        mov     rax, 60
        syscall

segment readable writeable
    msg db "Hello World!", 0xA
```

NASM

```
;will be set when compiling

section .text
    global _start
        _start:
            mov     rax, 1
            mov     rdi, 1
            lea     rsi, [msg]
            mov     rdx, 13
            syscall

            mov     rdi, 0
            mov     rax, 60
            syscall

section .data
    msg db " Hello World!", 0xA
```

As we can see, the actual commands are the same. What differs are the name and the way in which the individual program parts are defined as well as one or the other assembler-specific keyword and the way in which the assembler is told that he should build a 64-bit program.

In the case of FASM, the program gets converted into an executable as follows:

```
user@linuxpc: ~$ fasm hello_fasm.asm
```

With NASM you would have to perform the following two steps for that purpose:

```
user@linuxpc: ~$ nasm -f elf64 -o hello_nasm.o hello_nasm.asm
user@linuxpc: ~$ ld hello_fasm.o -o hello_nasm
```

FASM translates the program into an executable file with one single command.

NASM gets informed with `-f` that the output-format will be `elf64` (64-bit). With `-o` you define the name of the output object file and then you give it the path to the source code file as the last parameter. In a second step, you can then use `ld` or various other programs to create the executable program from the object file, here we are using again `-o` to specify the file name for the program.

We'll be using NASM in this book. Since neither building the executable programs in the command line nor developing (especially in assembly) without a debugger is really comfortable, we will also use a small but well-equipped IDE called SASM.

NASM can be downloaded at `https://www.nasm.us/` for Windows, DOS, OSX. Linux users can usually also install NASM with the respective package manager of the distribution (`apt`, `yum`, `dnf`, ...). On this occasion, you should also download the 284-page manual to have a reference for working with NASM.

As a reference for various background information and the commands of the i386 and x64 CPUs, I can recommend the Intel Software Developer Manual, which can be found at `https://software.intel.com/content/www/us/en/develop/articles/intel-sdm.html`.

You are welcome to use any other assembler as an exercise and then adapt the code accordingly. Do not forget to adjust the settings in SASM as well.

CPU-REGISTERS

Registers are data stores that the processor can access particularly quickly. With a 64-bit CPU, these have a width of 64-bit or 8 bytes of data. In addition, the 64-bit registers are divided into several sub-registers. Let's take a look at the example of the `rax` register:

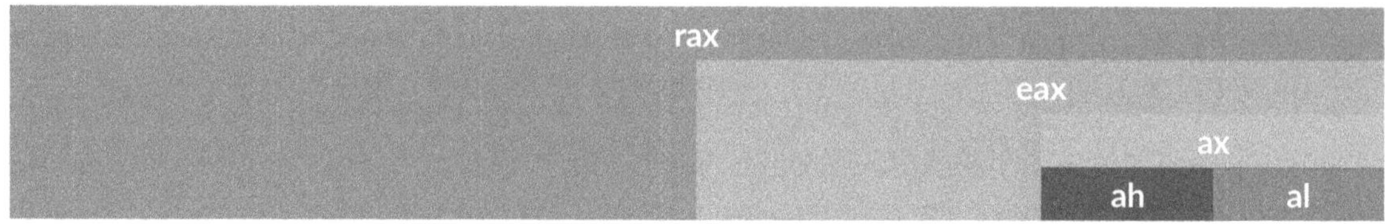

`rax` ... is the entire register with its 8 bytes of data (64-bit)
`eax` ... is the lower half of rax and corresponds to the old 4 byte registers (32-bit)
`ax` ... is the lower half of eax and corresponds to the old 2 byte registers (16-bit)
`ah` ... is the upper half of ax and can hold 1 byte of data (8-bit)
`al` ... is the lower half of ax and can hold 1 byte of data (8-bit)

This also ensures that older programs can run on newer CPU architectures. The basic instruction set of the CPUs has not changed since the 16-bit processors. Of course, new functions, special registers and instruction sets were always added, but the core instruction set remained the same.

Today we have the following registers:

Meaning	64-bit	32-bit	16-bit	8-bit high	8-bit low
Akkumulator	rax	eax	ax	ah	al
Base	rbx	ebx	bx	bh	bl
Counter	rcx	ecx	cx	ch	cl
Data	rdx	edx	dx	dh	dl
Source-Index	rsi	esi	si		
Destination-Index	rdi	edi	di		
General purpose register	r8	r8d	r8w		r8b
General purpose register	r9	r9d	r9w		r9b
General purpose register	r10	r10d	r10w		r10b
General purpose register	r11	r11d	r11w		r11b
General purpose register	r12	r12d	r12w		r12b
General purpose register	r13	r13d	r13w		r13b

Meaning	64-bit	32-bit	16-bit	8-bit high	8-bit low
General purpose register	r14	r14d	r14w		r14b
General purpose register	r15	r15d	r15w		r15b
Stack-Pointer	rsp	esp	sp		
Base-Pointer	rbp	ebp	bp		

The subdivision of the new registers r8-r15 looks like this - e.g. r8:

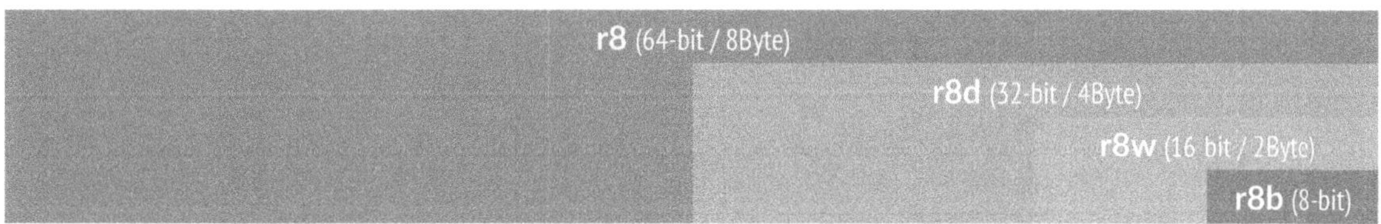

All these registers can be used in programs, but there are only a few cases in which the stack or base pointer, which should point to the top or bottom memory address of the stack, would have to be changed by hand. However, it is possible, but it can also be used to incorporate bugs, which are very difficult to find, into your program.

The following additional registers are also available, but can only be used indirectly:

Meaning	64-bit	32-bit	16-bit	8-bit high	8-bit low
Instruction-Pointer	rip	eip	ip		
Flags-Register	rflags	eflags	flags		

The instruction pointer cannot be changed directly and commands such as `mov rip, 0x1` lead to a `'rip' undefined symbol` error when compiling the program. The value of `rip`, `eip` or `ip` always points to the next instruction and is only changed or updated indirectly when an instruction is executed.

In addition to these general registers, there are other special registers for certain instruction sets, which we will not deal with in detail in this book:

```
FPU-Register    fpr0 - fpr7
MMX-Register    mmx0 - mmx7
SSE-Register    xmm0 - xmm15
```

THE FLAGS REGISTER

... is used to communicate certain states and events. These are evaluated by certain commands such as the conditional jump commands (`je`, `jne`, `jg`, `jl`, `jz`,...).

FLAGS				
Bit	Symbol	Name	1	0
0	CF	Carry Flag	carry	No carry
1		Reserved		
2	PF	Parity Flag	even	odd
3		Reserved		
4	AF	Auxiliary Carry Flag	Auxillery carry/borrow	No carry/borrow
5		Reserved		
6	ZF	Zero-Flag	Result was zero	Result was not zero
7	SF	Sign-Flag	Result was negative	Result was positive
8	TF	Trap-Flag		
9	IF	Interupt enable Flag	Interrupt activated	Interrupt deactivated
10	DF	Direction-Flag	Auto decrement	Auto increment
11	OF	Overflow-Flag	Overflow	No overflow
12, 13	IOPL	I/O Privilege Level		
14	NT	Nested Task Flag		
15		Reserved		
EFLAGS				
16	RF	Resume flag		
17	VM	Virtual 8086 mode Flag		
18	AC	Alignment Check		
19	VIF	Virtual Input Flag		
20	VIP	Virtual Interrupt Pending		
21	ID	CPIDI Instruction Flag		
22-31		Reserved		
RFLAGS				
32-63		Reserved		

Most flags are required for special applications, but we will take a closer look at the most important flags in the following chapter.

The flags register cannot be directly influenced either - at least most of it. Only a few bits can be set, reset or negated by hand.

This register or the bits in it are usually set when other commands are executed. In order to get a better idea of what exactly will happen, we will now take a closer look at the most important commands.

THE MAIN ASSEMBLY COMMANDS

In this chapter, we want to take a closer look at the most important commands and examine the mode of operation and the effects on the flags register in more detail.

We also want to deal with common stumbling blocks that repeatedly lead to all sorts of errors. Speaking of errors - these can be divided into the following three categories:

1) Syntax error
These errors occur when translating the program and they are very easy to find because the compiler / assembler / interpreter will criticize them directly and an error description usually will name us a line number in which the error occurred. - Please write the following program:

```
section .text
      global  _start
      _start:
            mow     rax, 1
```

As soon as you translate it with `user@linuxpc:~$` **nasm -f elf64 -o test.o test.asm** you get the following message:

```
test.asm: 6: error: parser: instruction expected
```

This is clear, because there is no `mow` command - it should be `mov`. NASM tries to inform us with `"instruction expected"` that there is no valid instruction at this point, although a valid instruction is requested.

So you see these errors are very easy to find. It becomes more difficult with the following two categories.

2) Runtime or runtime errors
In order to understand these errors more easily, we use the program shown above as follows:

```
section .text
      global  _start
      _start:
            mov     rax, 1
            mov     rbx, 0
            div     rbx
```

Now we can translate the program as shown before and we don't get any Error message.

Then we build the executable with `user@linuxpc:~$` **ld -o test test.o** and that will work as well. As soon as we run the program with `user@linuxpc:~$` **./test**, we get the following error:

```
Floating point exception (memory dump written)
```

So the program crashed at runtime and we don't exactly know in that case in which line the error occurred. Readers with programming experience have probably already guessed that we are producing a division by zero and this then leads to that error.

At least a memory dump, sometimes also called a core dump, is written. That could be analyzed. To learn how this is done in your system and where that files are stored, please check the manual of your distribution.

3) Logical errors
Are the worst category of errors and often very difficult to find. There is neither an error during compilation nor does the program crash during runtime. But it gives wrong or unexpected results.

We will go through such an example with the mathematical operators in which `1 + 2` suddenly results in `259`.

Debuggers are usually used to find runtime errors or logical errors. These tools are indispensable helpful for developers, without whom troubleshooting in many cases would hardly be possible!

Therefore, we will use SASM as an IDE from now on, because this tool also helps us to enter the code using syntax highlighting.

Open the test program from earlier in SASM and change a `mov` to `mow` and you will find that `mow` is shown in black and `mov` is shown in blue. The IDE tells us that way that `mov` is a command and `mow` is not. This is a way to quickly become aware of such errors based on typos.

TRANSFER AND FLAG COMMANDS

We have already worked with a few commands without explaining them. We will finally make up for that. Please write the following program in SASM:

```
section .text
    global  _start

    _start:
        ; set and exchange values
        mov     rax, 10
        mov     rbx, 20
        xchg    rax, rbx

        ; carry flag
        stc
        clc
        cmc
        cmc

        ; direction flag
        std
        cld

        ; exit
        mov     rax, 60
        mov     rdi, 0
        syscall
```

Save this program under any name and start the SASM debugger by clicking on the play symbol with the beetle shown below (framed in red):

With that, we start the debugger. You should now see the following window:

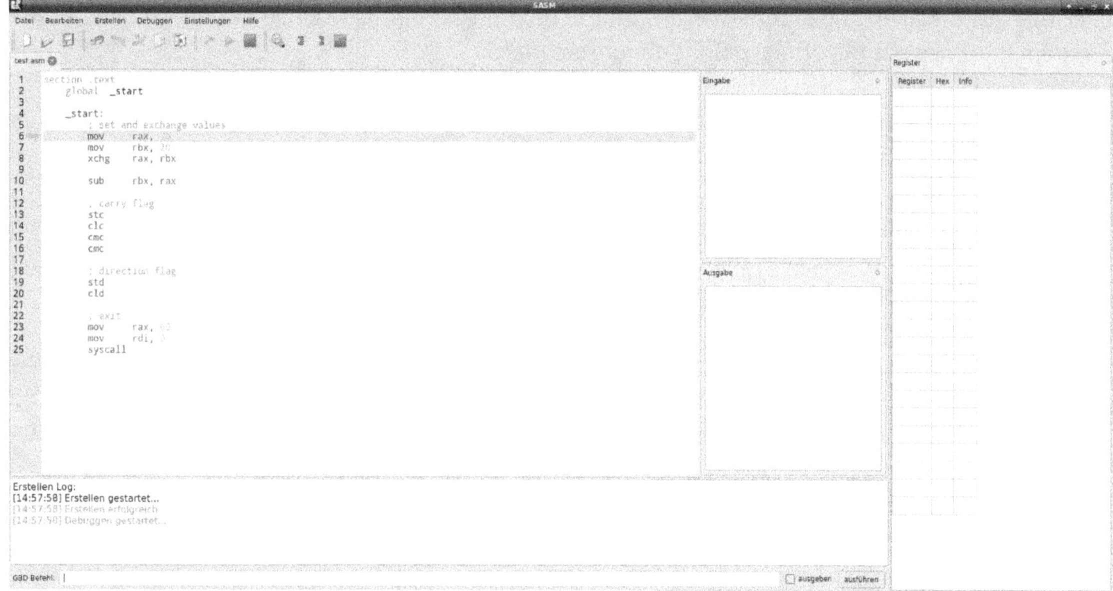

If you do not see the bar on the far right with the table of the registers then press Ctrl + R or click on Show registers in the Debug menu.

EXCURSUS DEBUGGING

As soon as you press the single-step button (framed in violet on the previous image), a line of code is executed and the registers update. In addition, the yellow bar that marks the current line moves down.

So we can look at the result of the previous line before we run the current line.

With the procedure step button, you can execute a function call throughout without going into the function as you would do with the single step.

With the stop button, we can cancel the execution. If we click on one of the line numbers in the gray left bar with the number, a red dot appears next to it. This is a so-called "breakpoint" at which the program stops. With a long program, you may want to look at a specific function and not always have to go through all the steps beforehand, and this is exactly why there are breakpoints.

After we started the debugger, the play symbol with the beetle became a circle with a beetle. If we click this button again, the program runs until the next breakpoint is reached or until the end of the program if it does not hit a breakpoint during execution.

The section `.text` line introduces the code part of the program. A program can have other parts in which additional data is stored. We'll take a closer look at these in later examples.

`global _start` defines the starting point of the program (the label `_start`) as global in order to avoid linker errors. The indentation of the lines that belong in a program part or further indentations to indicate the affiliation to a label is not necessary but they make a program more readable.

However, since you have to work a lot with jumps in assembly, you write code that is referred to as spaghetti code. Since it is not possible to avoid that due to the lack of better alternatives, you should make every effort to make things clearer so that you can find your way around the code more easily!

`_start:` is the label that marks the starting point of the program. With `ld` this should be called `_start` and when using `gcc` the label should be `_main`. So you can't just come up with some other name yourself.

All characters after a `;` are comments and get removed when the program is compiled. Comments are only notes and explanations that the programmer leaves for himself or others in the source code.

Now that you know how to work with the debugger, execute the first line and take a closer look at the registers.

You will see that the register `rax` now has the value `0xa` and in the `Info`-column you can see the value again in the decimal system as `10`. In addition, we see the eflags-Register has the value `0x202` and here too SASM helps us and displays it under Info as `[IF]` to show us that only the interrupt enable flag is set.

`mov rax, 10` moves the decimal value `10` into the `rax` register and is nothing more than the assignment of a value.

The registers can be compared with variables from other programming languages, only that these are fixed and you have to get by with the specified number and of course with the specified storage space the processor offers you.

When you execute the next line, the `rbx` register gets `0x14` or `20` assigned and no further flags are set.

`xchg rax, rbx` exchanges the values of `rax` and `rbx`. Also, no additionals flags get set by that command.

`stc` (set carry) sets the carry flag and now in the `eflags`-register row `[ CF  IF ]` get displayed.

`clc` (clear carry) deletes the carry flag.

The first `cmc` (complement carry) inverts the carry flags so it's set again. After the second `cmc` the carry flag disappears again.

`std` (set direction) sets the direction-flag and `cld` (clear direction) unsets it.

The following lines

```
mov rax, 60
mov rdi, 0
syscall
```

are used to end the program and to inform the operating system that the program has not crashed but was successfully ended. We will examine exactly what `syscalls` are in the next chapter. The next program we want to look at is this:

```
section .text
    global  _start

    _start:
        mov       al, 2
        mov       ah, 1
        cbw

        mov       eax, 0b10000000000000000
        mov       ax, 2
        cwde

        ; exit
        mov       rax, 60
        mov       rdi, 0
        syscall
```

Again, we will single-step through the program.

We already know the two `mov` commands, but let's take a closer look at what is happening in the registers:

`mov al, 2` sets the binary value `00000010` in register `al` (1 byte / 8 bit):

... ah			al								Result in ax / eax /rax
Bit	...	2	1	8	7	6	5	4	3	2	1	
Value	...	512	256	128	64	32	16	8	4	2	1	
	...	0	0	0	0	0	0	0	0	1	0	1 x 2 = 1

If we now use `mov ah, 1` to set the binary value `00000001` to register ah (1 byte / 8 bit), the `rax` register changes as follows:

... ah			al								Result in ax / eax /rax
Bit	...	2	1	8	7	6	5	4	3	2	1	
Value	...	512	256	128	64	32	16	8	4	2	1	
	...	0	1	0	0	0	0	0	0	1	0	1 x 256 + 1 x 2 = 258

For reasons of space we only considered the first 2 bits of ah. As we have already learned, ah and al are the upper and lower parts of ax and eax is the lower part of rax. Since we look at the entire rax register in the debugger, we get a total of 258 here.

If we execute cbw (convert byte to word) the al register is expanded to ax and the content of ah is overwritten by the new binary number `00000000 00000010`. An 8-bit value is also referred to as a byte, a 16-bit value as a word, a 32-bit value as a double word and a 64-bit value as a quad word.

Therefore, the debugger now shows 2 again as the value for rax.

With `mov eax, 0b10000000000000000` and `mov ax, 2` we create the same starting situation as before with ah and al - this time only with the registers eax and ax in a 16- and 32-bit context.

After these lines, there is the decimal value 65538 in rax. As soon as we now execute cwde (convert word to extended double) the same thing happens as before - the value of ax is expanded to eax and therefore the rax register is again set to 2.

ARITHMETIC COMMANDS

Next, let's look at the mathematical operations and the difficulties and problems that await us when working with the fixed bit values of the registers. We use the following program for this:

```
section .text
    global _start
    _start:
        mov rax, 100
        mov rbx, 200
        add rax, rbx

        mov al, 1
        mov bl, 2
        add rax, rbx

        mov rax, 100
        mov rbx, 200
        add al, bl

        mov rax, 100
        add al, bl
        adc ah, bh

        mov rax, 100
        mov rbx, 200
        sub al, bl

        mov rax, 100
        inc rax
        dec rax

        ; exit
        mov rax, 60
        mov rsi, 0
        syscall
```

First we assign the registers `rax` and `rbx` with `100` and `200` respectively and then `add` them up with `add rax, rbx` the result is saved in `rax`. This line can be understood as `rax = rax + rbx`.

Before we continue, let's have a look how the rax register looks like:

	... ah						al					Result in ax / eax /rax
Bit	...	2	1	8	7	6	5	4	3	2	1	
Value	...	512	256	128	64	32	16	8	4	2	1	
	...	0	1	0	0	1	0	1	1	0	0	256 + 32 + 8 + 4 = 300

As we can see, the number 300 no longer fits in the al-register because you can only cover the positive integers 1-255 with an 8-bit value. If we now load the bit pattern 00000001 into the al register with mov al, 1, the ah register remains unaffected:

	... ah						al					Result in ax / eax /rax
Bit	...	2	1	8	7	6	5	4	3	2	1	
Value	...	512	256	128	64	32	16	8	4	2	1	
	...	0	1	0	0	0	0	0	0	0	1	256 + 1 = 257

Therefore, the debugger now shows 257 as a value in rax and not 1. If we now put the decimal number 2 in the register bl, we get the number 2 as a result in the entire rbx register. This is because the number 200 (binary 11001000) can be represented in 8-bit and therefore no further bits have been set in the larger registers.

If we add rax and rbx in the expectation that we calculate 1 + 2, the result of 259 will surprise us. Here it is obvious, since we deliberately provoke this mistake, but in practice a forgotten mov rax, 0 or xor rax, rax can cause quite a bit of a headache!

The CPU usually does nothing for you automatically in the background, so if you do not make sure yourself that the entire 64 bits of the rax register have been zeroed and simply re-assign the lowest byte of the register and then suddenly work with the entire register again, the respective operation will also work with bits remaining in the higher bytes from previous operations.

Let's look at the reverse case by overwriting the entire register with mov rax, 100 and mov rbx, 200. Then we add the lowest 8 bits with add al, bl and save the result in al. Now the debugger shows us the value of 44 instead of 300:

	... ah						al					Result in ax / eax /rax
Bit	...	2	1	8	7	6	5	4	3	2	1	
Value	...	512	256	128	64	32	16	8	4	2	1	
	...	0	X	0	0	1	0	1	1	0	0	32 + 8 + 4 = 44

As we know, the number `300` no longer fits in an 8-bit register.

However, since we are now explicitly working with 8-bit registers, the processor will prevent such an overflow from damaging the data which could be in the `ah` register and therefore the overflowing bits are simply cut off - represented by the X here. However, the `eflags` register points this out because the carry flag (`CF`) is now set.

That is also the only clue we get. In the previous example, we didn't even have this hint!

So let's see how you can work with the `CF`.

With `mov rax, 100` and `add al, bl` bring us again the same situation and we have set the `CF` and again as well as our wrong result of 44 but this code-block has an additional line:

```
adc ah, bh
```

As soon as run this, line the `rax` register has the correct result: `300`. `adc` (add with carry) is used if the result no longer fit in one register. In that case, the bit pattern of the number can be divided into 2 registers.

Here we used `al` and `bl` for the lower bits and `ah` and `bh` for the upper bits and then performed the addition in 2 steps. Since we are using smaller registers here, the debugger in `rax` immediately shows us the correct result and of course, we could switch to `ax` if `al` became to small or to `eax` if the number range of `ax` is no longer sufficient, but what if not even `rax` is insufficient to represent a number or a result? This is exactly when this technique comes into play!

Here form `dx:ax` and `bx:cx` or `edx:eax` and `ebx:ecx` or `rdx:rax` and `rbx:rcx` pairs for the higher or lower bits. So we can combine 2 registers into one and perform the addition in 2 steps.

Then we use `mov rax, 100` and `mov rbx, 200` to put the values `100` and `200` in the registers and subtract the `bl` value of `al` with `sub al, bl` and save the result in `al`. The `eflags` register changes again and now shows the Sign Flag (`SF`), among other things.

`sub` also follows the same scheme as `add` and could be represented as `rax = rax - rbx`. This time we get the value is `156` in rax displayed.

The sign flag changes the way the value is read. If we had executed `sub rax, rbx`, the debugger would display the value correctly and apply the sign flag to the entire register. However, I would not be able to represent this long bit sequence in this way.

So here we do it manually - first we need the binary representation of `156`:

```
>>> bin(156)
'0b10011100'
```

Then we enter this bit-pattern in our well-known register grid. What is new here is that the highest bit no longer stands for 128 but for -128:

... ah			al								Result in ax / eax /rax
Bit	...	2	1	8	7	6	5	4	3	2	1	
Value	...	512	256	-128	64	32	16	8	4	2	1	
	...	0	0	1	0	0	1	1	1	0	0	-128 + 16 + 8 + 4 = -100

That is how signed numbers work...

With signed numbers, the highest bit represents its value as a negative number. The SASM debugger apparently only performs this operation if we use the entire register in the operation where the sign flag is set ...

Finally, we overwrite `rax` with the number 100 and as we can see, the SF is still set here too, an `xor rax, rax` would have reset the SF. So we always have to pay attention to such details and under certain circumstances make sure that we reset the flags accordingly when we no longer need them!

The `inc rax` (increment) increases the value of `rax` by one and now the debugger shows the value of 101 in the info field. At the same time, the parity flag (PF) was set in the eflags register to indicate that this number is odd.

`dec rax` (decrement) decreases the value of `rax` by one.

Next, we want to take a look at the `cmp` operator and we use this program:

```nasm
section .text
    global  _start

    _start:
        mov rax, 100
        mov rbx, 100
        sub rax, rbx

        mov rax, 100
        inc rax
        dec rax
        cmp rax, rbx

        ; exit
        mov rax, 60
        mov rdi, 0
        syscall
```

After we have executed `mov rax, 100` and `mov rbx, 100` and `sub rax, 100`, the rax register is set to 0, the rbx register to 100 and the eflags register to `[PF ZF IF]`.

So far this is not a real surprise except for the parity register which shows an "odd" 0. At this point, I do not want to discuss whether this is a bug or a feature on my Ryzen 2700 (2nd gen.).

With `mov rax, 100` we restore the initial value, the `inc rax` clears the ZF and the `dec rax` the PF so that we then get only `[IF]` in the eflags register. This would bring us back to the state before the `sub rax, rbx`.

Now if we let `cmp rax, rbx` run, the eflags register shows again `[PF ZF IF]` but now the 100 is still in rax. The cmp (compare) operator does exactly the same as sub, but discards the result and only sets the flags so that we can react to them with the appropriate jump commands.

Incidentally, you could also write `cmp rax, 100` - with cmp the second parameter can also be a number ...

To look at the division and multiplication of values we use the following program:

```asm
section .text
    global  _start

    _start:
        mov   al, 11
        mov   bl, 5
        div   bl

        mov   ax, 11
        div   bx

        mov   dx, 100
        ;mov   dx, 0    ; Keep that commented out!!!
        mov   ax, 33
        div   bx

        mov   ax, 10
        mov   bx, 20
        mul   bx

        mov   ax, 10
        mov   bx, 20
        imul  bl

        ; exit
        mov   rax, 60
        mov   rdi, 0
        syscall
```

Which we examine as usual with the debugger ...

When dividing, the dividend (the number to be divided) must be in al, ax, eax or rax. The divisor can be in any other register. We used bl here. The command div bl (divide) corresponds to ax = al / bl. The entire ax register is used for the result. As soon as we execute the line, we receive 0x102 or 258 in the debugger. This is not a mistake! To explain the behavior, let's take a closer look at the bit pattern of 258:

```
>>> bin (258)
'0b100000010'
```

and enter this in our bit grid:

	... ah			al								Result in ax / eax /rax
Bit	...	2	1	8	7	6	5	4	3	2	1	
Value	...	512	256	-128	64	32	16	8	4	2	1	
	...	0	1	0	0	0	0	0	0	1	0	256 + 2 = 258

What the debugger doesn't know is how to interpret the result. The processor works like a primary school student - in al we save the result and in ah the rest.

If we now consider this from this point of view, al contains the bit pattern 00000010 and ah the bit pattern 00000001 - if we calculate the decimal values we get:

```
>>> int("0b00000010", 2)
2
>>> int("0b00000001", 2)
1
```

11 devided by 5 = 2 and 1 rest.

If we now restore the previous state with mov ax, 11 and now divide with 16-bit values as when calling div bx, we get a different picture: In rxa there is now 2 and in rdx there is 1. This is because from 16-bit the result is divided into the corresponding accumulator and data registers - i.e. ax and dx, eax and edx or rax and rdx depending on the bit depth we are working with.

Now if we run mov dx, 100 and mov ax, 33 to fill these registers with new values and then execute the div bx command again, we would expect to divide 33 by 5 but we get instead the error "Program received signal SIGFPE, Arithmetic exception".

Stop execution at this point and comment out mov dx, 100 by typing one ; before the command or remove this line. We'll see what happens here. Leave mov dx, 0 commented out and run the program again!

Now we do not get an error, but the result is now 13113 and 4 remainder. That cannot be right either, And this time the manual interpretation of the bit patterns does not help us either. If a number is too large for a register, you can split it and put the higher bits in the data register and the lower bits in the accumulator register. Again, you can use the ax and dx, eax and edx or rax and rdx as pairs to mimic a bigger register.

So we don't divide 33 in the ax register (00000000 00100001), but the number that gives the following bit pattern:

dx: 00000000 00000001 + **ax:** 00000000 00100001 = 00000000 00000001 00000000 00100001

For the sake of clarity, I have separated the bit patterns by bytes. We have to undo that for Python. So let's use Python to convert that into a decimal number:

```
>>> int("0b00000000000000000100000000000100001", 2)
65569
```

Now the result makes sense again because 65569/5 = 13113 and 4 rest! The arithmetic error from earlier also means that the result no longer fits in the register. Since we divide a fairly large number (6,553,633) by a fairly small one, we get a result that by no means fits into the 16-bit of the ax register.

You can convert the numbers for the case yourself as an exercise and check how I came to $6,553,633$. As you can see, it is very important to check whether the corresponding data register is empty or not so that we can get the appropriate results.

If you want you can now remove the comment character before `mov dx, 0` and restart the program - you will then see that `rax` contains the number 6 and `rdx` the 3 after propper cleanup before the next division.

`mov ax, 10` and `mov bx, 20` sets the two numerical values and `mul bx` calculates `ax = ax * bx`. If we now look at the `rdx` register, we will notice that suddenly `rdx` is back to 0. This is because `mul` splits the result and, in the case of `ax`, stores the higher bits in `dx` and the lower bits in `ax`. A 16-bit multiplication delivers a 32-bit value split up into two 16-bit registers!

You are welcome to try this yourself by running:

```
mov ax, 1000
mov bx, 2000
mul bx
```

Then you get the value 33920 in `ax` and the value 30 in `dx`. The CF is also set to notify you that the result has been split up in two registers.

Again, you can use Python to generate and then assemble the bit patterns - if you do it right, you will get the expected 2 million as a result!

`mov ax, 10` and `mov bx, 10` restore the initial state. This time we use `imul` (Signed Integer Multiply) instead of `mul` and we get the 200 in `rax` again but here the CF and the OF are set. Because `imul` works with sign-based values, there is an overflow. Let's take a look at the value range of a signed 8-bit value:

	... ah			al								Result in ax / eax / rax
Bit	...	2	1	8	7	6	5	4	3	2	1	
Value	...	512	256	-128	64	32	16	8	4	2	1	
max.	...	0	0	0	1	1	1	1	1	1	1	64+32+16+8+4+2+1=127
min.	...	0	0	1	0	0	0	0	0	0	0	-128+0=-128
	...	0	0	1	1	0	0	1	0	0	0	-128+64+8=-56

I hope with this illustration of the bit patterns in the registers it becomes clear what the value range of a signed 8-bit integer is and how these numbers work. The bit pattern for 200 (11001000) entered in the grid shown above results in -56 when interpreted as signed value. And therefore CF and OF warn us that the calculated value cannot be displayed. If we simply continued to work with the value without paying attention to the flags, then we would continue to work with an incorrect value if we work with an operation that takes the sign into account. If we then treated the value as an unsigned integer, further calculations would be correct again.

Similar to `imul`, there are also `idiv` for the division of signed numbers.

The difficulty in assembly is that we are responsible for ensuring that values are interpreted in the right way. Apart from that, an overflow can lead to incorrect results in calculations. Therefore we have to pay attention to the flags and react accordingly when a CF or OF is set.

LOGICAL OPERATORS

Logical operators work bitwise and thus show how a processor works. The CPU is nothing more than an enormous accumulation of circuits through which current pulses are passing. One part of that impulses (the command) manipulates the path that the other part of the impulses (the data) take.

There are some projects and many good videos on Youtube about how to build an 8-bit computer on several breadboards and corresponding sets with all components. For anyone who wants to understand the structure of a CPU better, I recommend **Ben Eater**'s videos:

```
https://www.youtube.com/watch?v=HyznrdDSSGM&list=PLowKtXNTBypGqImE405J2565dvjafglHU
```

To look at these operators, I wrote the following program:

```
section .text
    global  _start

    _start:
        mov al, 11
        not al
        shl al, 2
        shr al, 2
        neg al

        mov al, 28
        mov bl, 120
        and al, bl

        mov al, 28
        or  al, bl

        mov al, 28
        xor al, bl

        ; exit
        mov rax, 60
        mov rdi, 0
        syscall
```

...which we will debug.

With `mov al, 11` we put the bit pattern shown below into the register.

	... ah			al								Result in ax / eax / rax
Bit	...	2	1	8	7	6	5	4	3	2	1	
Value	...	512	256	128	64	32	16	8	4	2	1	
mov	...	0	0	0	0	0	0	1	0	1	1	8 + 1 + 1 = 11
not	...	0	0	1	1	1	1	0	1	0	0	128 + 64 + 32 + 16 + 4 = 244

The `not` operator works again as `al = not al` and that for saves the result in `al`. All bits are negated - a 0 becomes a 1 and vice versa. You can see this very well above.

The `shl` (shift left) operator expects 2 arguments - the register and the number of places by which the bits get shifted. After the `not` operation we have the number 244 in al or rax.

	... ah			al								Result in ax / eax / rax
Bit	...	2	1	8	7	6	5	4	3	2	1	
Value	...	512	256	128	64	32	16	8	4	2	1	
not	...	0	0	1	1	1	1	0	1	0	0	128 + 64 + 32 + 16 + 4 = 244
shl	...	X	X	1	1	0	1	0	0	0	0	128 + 64 + 16 = 208

After the `shl` operation we get the number 208 in the register and CF, AF and SF were set because we cut off the two highest bits - shown here as X in the ah register. It is important to note that the bits are not simply shifted into the next larger register! If there is no overflow when bits are omitted, a `shl` by one digit is the same as a multiplication by 2 and `shl` by two digits works like multiplying by 4, etc.

You can see that in the `shr` (shift right) operation. This shifts the bytes two places to the right and corresponds to the division by 4 in this example:

	... ah			al								Result in ax / eax / rax
Bit	...	2	1	8	7	6	5	4	3	2	1	
Value	...	512	256	128	64	32	16	8	4	2	1	
shl	...	0	0	1	1	0	1	0	0	0	0	128 + 64 + 16 = 208
shr	...	0	0	0	0	1	1	0	1	0	0	32 + 16 + 4 = 52

Hereby the CF, AF and SF get deleted.

Like not, shr, and shl, the neg (negate) command corresponds to the pattern al = neg al.

	... ah			al								Result in ax / eax / rax
Bit	...	2	1	8	7	6	5	4	3	2	1	
Value	...	512	256	128	64	32	16	8	4	2	1	
shr	...	0	0	0	0	1	1	0	1	0	0	32 + 16 + 4 = 52
neg	...	0	0	1	1	0	0	1	1	0	0	-128 + 64 + 8 + 4 = -52

The bits are rearranged in such a way that, when treated as a signed number, the new value will be the old one multiplied by -1. So 52 becomes -52 and -52 becomes 52. Don't get confused just because the debugger displays 204. He just misinterprets the number!

In this case neg also sets the sign flag.

The following operators take 2 arguments and therefore we look at the al and bl regiser and the result of the command, which is then saved again in al.

These operators also work bit by bit, but considering the numerical values makes little sense in the following cases. I just broken them down so that you can better track what's going on with the displayed values in the debugger.

The following operators are purely intended to manipulate bit patterns and not really used to do some math!

The and command is the logical AND combination of two values.

	... ah/bh			al/bl								Result in ax / eax / rax
Bit	...	2	1	8	7	6	5	4	3	2	1	
Value	...	512	256	128	64	32	16	8	4	2	1	
al	...	0	0	0	0	0	1	1	1	0	0	16 + 8 + 4 = 28
bl	...	0	0	0	1	1	1	1	0	0	0	64 + 32 + 16 + 8 = 120
and	...	0	0	0	0	0	1	1	0	0	0	16 + 8 = 24

The result is 1 if the respective bit contains a 1 in both registers. In all other cases the result is 0.

The exact opposite of this is the logical OR operation or the or command:

	... ah/bh			al/bl								Result in ax / eax /rax
Bit	...	2	1	8	7	6	5	4	3	2	1	
Value	...	512	256	128	64	32	16	8	4	2	1	
al	...	0	0	0	0	0	1	1	1	0	0	16 + 8 + 4 = 28
bl	...	0	0	0	1	1	1	1	0	0	0	64 + 32 + 16 + 8 = 120
or	...	0	0	0	1	1	1	1	1	0	0	64 + 32 + 16 + 8 + 4 = 124

Here the result is a 0 if there is a 0 in both registers at the respective position and in any other case the result is a 1.

The third logical link is the exclusive-or which we use with the xor operator:

	... ah/bh			al/bl								Result in ax / eax /rax
Bit	...	2	1	8	7	6	5	4	3	2	1	
Value	...	512	256	128	64	32	16	8	4	2	1	
al	...	0	0	0	0	0	1	1	1	0	0	16 + 8 + 4 = 28
bl	...	0	0	0	1	1	1	1	0	0	0	64 + 32 + 16 + 8 = 120
xor	...	0	0	0	1	1	0	0	1	0	0	64 + 32 + 4 = 100

Here you get a 1 for different bits and a 0 where the bits match.

This also explains why mov rax, 0 and xor rax, rax both fill the rax register with zeros. Which variant you should use in which case also depends on whether you want to reset the CF, PF and AF flags or not. xor sets these flags to 0, mov leaves the flags untouched!

VARIOUS OTHER COMMANDS

One command that we have seen but not explained is `lea` (load effective address). In the FASM and NASM comparison, we have used that command to load the memory address of the label `text` into a register.

The syntax here is, for example, `lea  rax,  [label]` whereby the memory address of a label is loaded into the register `rax`. The label must be enclosed in [ ].

We'll look at the `syscall` (system call) and `int` (interrupt) operator in the following chapter.

The `nop` (no operation) command tells the processor to do nothing and is especially popular with exploit code to increase the target that you want to hit with the `rip` or `eip`.

We'll look at all the jump commands (`call`, `ret` and the entire `j` family) in detail in the "functions and branches" section. The same applies to the `push` and `pop` family!

HELLO WORLD IN NASM

Now let's take a closer look at how the "Hello world" example works. Since I have already explained the `lea` operator, I want to show you a way that works in NASM - but be careful, if you work with FASM, the commands `equ $-text` and `mov rsi, text` will cause an error or work differently!

But let's first look at the code example:

```
section .data
    text        db "Hello World!", 0xA
    len         equ $-text

section .text
    global      _start

    _start:
        mov         rax, 1
        mov         rdi, 1
        mov         rsi, text
        mov         rdx, len
        syscall

        ; exit
        mov         rax, 60
        mov         rdi, 0
        syscall
```

This is because NASM understands that we mean `lea rsi, [text]` when we wrote `mov rsi, text` and exchange the commands correctly when translating. FASM does not do that.

`equ` gives a numeric constant a name. This is nothing more than a label. We will take a closer look at our own labels in the next chapter and then it should become clearer.

What is NASM-specific here is the `$-text`, which means nothing other than the beginning of the actual line ($) minus the start address of `text`. If you remember, the text was simply packed into the binary file after the actual commands:

```
000000b0: b8 01 00 00 00 bf 01 00 00 00 48 be dc 00 60 00   ..........H...`.
000000c0: 00 00 00 00 ba 0d 00 00 00 0f 05 eb 02 eb e1 b8   ................
000000d0: 3c 00 00 00 bf 00 00 00 00 0f 05 00 48 65 6c 6c   <...........Hell
000000e0: 6f 20 57 6f 72 6c 64 21 0a 00 00 00 00 00 00 00   o World!........
000000f0: 00 00 00 00 00 00 00 00 00 00 00 00 00 00 00 00   ................
```

So we are basically after the 0a (which in the ASCII table corresponds to the newline character or a line break) and the label `text` points to the character 48 (what stands for the H in the ASCII table).

Now let's take Python and do the math:

```
>>> int ("e9", 16) - int ("dc", 16)
13
```

... if you are wondering how I come up with e9 and dc - the character 6f corresponds to the address e0, the space (20) corresponds to the address e1, etc. You only need to count to the corresponding position in the hexadecimal system.

The reason why a 0d (hexadecimal for 13) cannot be found immediately afterward is that the named constants are stored elsewhere in the program. `equ` defines the constant for the preprocessor which hardcode the numeric value into the binary.

I also put the `.data` segment at the beginning of the program to show that the program parts can also be placed in the source code in different orders.

Now let's take a look at the core of this exercise - the system calls!

SYSTEM CALLS

... or syscalls for short allow the program to issue a command to the operating system. When a program is running in an operating system, it cannot simply send data to the graphics card to draw some text on the screen.

The operating system has to take care that the requests to various system components such as hard disks, graphics cards, etc. do not get in the way of other requests of other programs. Further, it would be extremely complex to pack the controls for all possible graphics cards in one program and you would need to update your program always when a new graphics card gets released.

We, therefore, provide the operating system the necessary data in the registers and then pass control to the operating system with the `syscall` command so that the OS can process our request.

In a 64-bit Linux system, the registers would be assigned as follows:

Syscall-ID	Param. 1	Param. 2	Param. 3	Param. 4	Param. 5	Param. 6
rax	rdi	rsi	rdx	r10	r8	r9

The return value of the system call gets stored in `rax`.

EXCURSUS - 32-BIT ASSEMBLY

On a 32-bit Linux system you have to set the registers as follows:

Syscall-ID	Param. 1	Param. 2	Param. 3	Param. 4	Param. 5	Param. 6
eax	ebx	ecx	edx	esi	edi	ebp

Here, too, the return value ends up in the accumulator register (eax).

This is also one of the cases where you have to change the base pointer if necessary. Before that, you should put it on top of the stack and then load it from there again. But we'll take a closer look at the stack in the next chapter. To call the system call, the command `int 80h` (interrupt) was used for 32-bit instead of the `syscall` command.

SYSCALLS AND THEIR PARAMETERS

You will be wondering where you got the syscall numbers and their parameters from. To do this, you can simply search for this header file on your Linux system using the `locate unistd_64.h` terminal command.

You will find some versions of it, the path should look like this:

```
/usr/src/linux-headers-5.3.0-53-generic/arch/x86/include/generated/uapi/asm/unistd_64.h
```

Of course, the kernel version will be different for you ...

If we open this file in any editor, you should see the following:

```
#ifndef _ASM_X86_UNISTD_64_H
#define _ASM_X86_UNISTD_64_H 1

#define __NR_read 0
#define __NR_write 1
#define __NR_open 2
#define __NR_close 3
#define __NR_stat 4
#define __NR_fstat 5
... etc.
```

Incidentally, the file `unistd_32.h` is responsible for 32-bit.

In it, we see that the system call number 1 stands for `write`. As soon as we enter `man 2 write` in a terminal we can see the following:

```
WRITE(2)                    Linux Programmer's Manual                    WRITE(2)

NAME
       write - write to a file descriptor

SYNOPSIS
       #include <unistd.h>

       ssize_t write(int fd, const void *buf, size_t count);
       ... etc.
```

These manuals can also be read more conveniently, for example on the website `https://man7.org`.

Here we are told that the `write` function expects three parameters:

1. the file-descriptor (`fd`)
2. a pointer to the memory address in which the text is located (`* buf`) and
3. the length of the string (`count`)

The return value is the number of bytes written. This also explains why the `rax` register is set to 13 after the Syscall.

Armed with this knowledge, we can now almost completely decipher the Syscall:

```
mov         rax, 1          ; write
mov         rdi, 1          ; fd
mov         rsi, text       ; *buf
mov         rdx, len        ; count
```

Now the only question is where we get the file descriptor from. In Linux, three file descriptors are already predefined: 0 stands for `stdin`, 1 for `strout` and 2 for `stderr`. Further, we can get a different file descriptor from a previous `open` syscall.

If we continue to search in the `unistd_64.h` file, we will find the following line:

```
#define __NR_exit 60
```

`man 2 exit` will show us:

```
_EXIT(2)                    Linux Programmer's Manual                    EXIT(2)


NAME
       _exit, _Exit - terminate the calling process

SYNOPSIS
       #include <unistd.h>

       void _exit(int status);
       ... ect.
```

The `exit` Syscall requires one parameter - the numeric status code with which the program was ended. In Linux, the 0 stands for "Everything OK" and a different number would be an error code with which the program was ended.

BRANCHES IN ASSEMBLER

Readers with programming experience know different constructs from other languages to react to certain events or circumstances in the program.

In assembly we have the commands of the jump-family. Let's take a look at the commands that are included:

jmp   jump (always executed, this is an unconditional jump)

je   Jump if Equal
jz   Jump if Zero-flag is set
jp   Jump if Parity-flag is set
jpe   Jump if Parity-flag show Even
jne   Jump if Not Equal
jnz   Jump if Not set Zero-flag
jnp   Jump if Not set Parity-flag
jpo   Jump if Parity-flag show Odd
jcxz   Jump if 16-bit Counter-register is Zero (cx)
jecxz   Jump if Extended Counter-register is Zero (ecx)

The other so-called conditional jumps are divided into those that evaluate the result of a previous cmp command as if the compared values were unsigned or signed numbers.

UNSINED JUMPS

ja   Jump if Above
jae   Jump if Above or Equal
jb   Jump if Below
jbe   Jump if Below or Equal
jna   Jump if Not Above
jnae   Jump if Not Above or Equal
jnb   Jump if Not Below
jnbe   Jump if Not Below or Equal
jc   Jump if Carry-flag is set
jnc   Jump if Not set Carry-flag

SIGNED JUMPS

```
jg      Jump if Greater
jge     Jump if Greater or Equal
jl      Jump if Less
jle     Jump if Less or Equal
jng     Jump if Not Greater
jnge    Jump if Not Greater or Equal
jnl     Jump if Not Less
jnle    Jump if Not Less or Equal
jo      Jump if Overflow-flag is set
jno     Jump if Not set Overflow-flag
js      Jump if Sign-flag is set
jns     Jump if Not set Sign-flag
```

The syntax for all jumps is `jmp address` but since we prefer to leave the calculation of the addresses to the assembler, we usually use lables.

A label is a freely defined text that ends with an `:`. The same rules apply for this as for variables in different programming languages. Use only the characters `A-Z, 0-9` and the underscore, but no other special characters. Besides, labels are case-sensitive, meaning that they differentiate between upper and lower case. `_yes` and `_Yes` are therefore two different labels for NASM.

Let's look at the following example code:

```
section .data
    is10    db  "RAX is 10", 0xA
    lenIs   equ $-is10

    not10   db  "RAX is not 10", 0xA
    lenNot  equ $-not10

section .text
    global  _start

    _start:
        ; setup values for comparison
        mov     rax, 10
        mov     rbx, 10
```

```asm
    ; compare
    cmp     rax, rbx
    je      _yes
    jmp     _no

_yes:
    ; set text + len for syscall
    mov     rsi, is10
    mov     rdx, lenIs
    jmp     _end

_no:
    ; set text + len for syscall
    mov     rsi, not10
    mov     rdx, lenNot

_end:
    ; rest of write-syscall
    mov     rax, 1
    mov     rdi, 1
    syscall

    ; end programm
    mov     rax, 60
    mov     rdi, 0
    syscall
```

First, we define two string in the `.data` section which we can address with `is10` and `not10` and the associated text lengths as named constants `lenIs` and `lenNot`.

Then we set `rax` and `rbx` to the value `10`.

The `cmp` command compares `rax` and `rbx` and sets the `eflags` register accordingly. Then the zero flag is evaluated. So the command does exactly the same thing as `jz` that is not an error, but should serve clarity and underline the comparison. `jz` or `jcxz` would be more suitable for a counting loop.

Assembler with its cryptic mnemonics and its syntax is very confusing and difficult to understand, compared to other programming languages. Especially because the simplest programs are much longer than in other languages.

For comparison, the same program in Python:

```python
value = 10
serched_value = 10

if value == serched_value:
    print("RAX is 10")
else:
    print("RAX is not 10")
```

You can write this program not only shorter but also much more understandable because `if value == serched_value` says much more clearly what is going on then `cmp rax, rbx` and `jmp label`!

Besides, the meaningful naming of variables provides further clarity. In assembler we mostly deal with registers and we can only name the labels meaningfully. Therefore, you should as much as possible make sure to set at least meaningful labels and jump commands that also underline the meaning of the program.

Labels don't have to be short - inspired by Austin Powers you could name your lables like that:

```
je     _yes_yes_yes_the_register_rax_is_10_yeah_baby_groovie
jmp    _oh_no_shame_on_me_i_dont_set_rbx_to_10
```

But back to our program - after `cmp` has set the flags, we will jump to the `_yes` label if `rax` and `rbx` both have the value 10. In `_yes` the pointer to the string at the label `is10` and the length of this text is loaded into `rsi` and `rdx`. The `jmp _end` then ensures that we skip the `_no` part. If we didn't do this, the contents of `rsi` and `rdx` would be overwritten and the output would be wrong.

If you have changed any of the values, no jump is made in the line `je _yes` and `jmp _no` ensures that we then jump directly to `_no`. And set the values provided in it.

Since the label `_end` comes immediately after the code of `_no`, we can save ourselves a `jmp _end` at this point.

In `_end`, we set `rax` and `rdi` to 1 to complete the `write` system call, and `syscall` finally triggers the output. This is followed by the well-known `exit` system call.

Now you maybe understand why this is called spaghetti code?

The example also shows another problem. Another developer may not need to know that `rbx` contains the value it was looking for, and he could change `rbx`. Then RAX is not 10 would be output, even if the value 10 is stored in `rax`. A comment for explanation or the comparison `cmp rax, 10` would remedy the situation!

As you can see, it is not easy to write selfexplainatory assembly code.

To investigate the difference between signed and unsigned jumps, you could simply change the following lines:

```
    ; setup values for comparison
    mov     rax, 10
    mov     rbx, 129

    ; compare
    cmp     al, bl
    ja      _yes
    jmp     _no
```

As an exercise, I let you examine for yourself what is output in the case of `ja` and `jg`. You should possibly also adjust the texts that are outputting so that a correspondingly meaningful text is outputted.

LOOPS AND FUNCTIONS IN ASSEMBLY

Now let's take a look at another example program in which we combine the previously learned with
loop constructions and the use of the stack:

```
section .data
    digit   db   " is a digit", 0xA
    lenDig  equ $-digit

    number  db   " is a number", 0xA
    lenNum  equ $-number

    errNan  db   "Just positive numbers are allowed!", 0xA
    lenNan  equ $-errNan

    prompt  db   "Enter a number: "
    lenPro  equ $-prompt

    lenInp  equ 20

section .bss
    ; reserve space for user input
    input   resb lenInp

section .text
    global  _start

    _start:
        ; output prompt
        mov     rax, 1
        mov     rdi, 1
        mov     rsi, prompt
        mov     rdx, lenPro
        syscall

        ; get user input
        mov     rax, 0
        mov     rdi, 0
        mov     rsi, input
        mov     rdx, lenInp
        syscall
```

```asm
        ;call    _fakeSyscall

        ; count input length and calc. value of string
        mov     rax, 0
        mov     rbx, 10                     ; base 10 for converting
        mov     rcx, 0
        mov     rdx, 0

_count_len_loop:
        mov     rax, rdx                    ; load last sum (RDX) into RAX
                                            ; for multiplication with 10
        mul     rbx                         ; multiply RAX with 10
        mov     dl, byte [input + rcx]      ; get byte into DL

        cmp     dl, 48
        jb      _errorNan                   ; jump if below
        cmp     dl, 57
        ja      _errorNan                   ; jump if above

        sub     rdx, 48                     ; subtract 48 to convert ascii
                                            ; to integer
        add     rdx, rax                    ; RAX + RDX  => 0 * 10 + 1 = 1
                                            ;               1 * 10 + 2 = 12
                                            ;              12 * 10 + 3 = 123

        inc     rcx                         ; increment counter for output
        cmp     byte [input + rcx], 0xA     ; check for newline char
        jne     _count_len_loop             ; continue counting if next byte
                                            ; is not newline-character

        ; store int value of input on stack
        push    rdx

        ; output number
        mov     rax, 1
        mov     rdi, 1
        mov     rsi, input
        mov     rdx, rcx                     ; counter value from before
        syscall
```

```nasm
        ; setup values for comparison
        pop     rax                                     ; get int value from stack back

        ; compare
        cmp     rax, 10
        jb      _isDigit                                ; jump if below

    _isNumber:
        ; set text + len for syscall
        mov     rsi, number
        mov     rdx, lenNum
        jmp     _end

    _isDigit:
        ; set text + len for syscall
        mov     rsi, digit
        mov     rdx, lenDig
        jmp     _end

    _errorNan:
        ; set text + len for syscall
        mov     rsi, errNan
        mov     rdx, lenNan

    _end:
        ; rest of syscall and do output result
        mov     rax, 1
        mov     rdi, 1
        syscall

        ; end programm
        mov     rax, 60
        mov     rdi, 0
        syscall


_fakeSyscall:
    mov     rax, input
    mov     [rax], dword 0x0A333231 ; store 123\n in input (little endian)
    ret
```

As you can see, assembly programs quickly get longer. I have commented on the program for you in more detail than I would normally do so that you can follow the code even better.

The .data section hardly needs any explanation, except that here we use lenInp equ 20 to create a named constant called lenInp to which we assign the decimal number 20.

What is new here is the .bss section, in which storage space is reserved, which we will fill later. This can be compared to creating an empty variable. More precisely, 20 bytes of memory are made available with resb 20 (reserve bytes) and this is given the label input.

At the beginning of _start we have our write system call again, which outputs the text from Label prompt. The read system call is new here. This has the ID 0 (rax), gets the file descriptor 0 (stdin) in rdi, the pointer to the storage space (input) in rsi and the length (lenInp) in rdx.

This is followed by a commented-out line of code with which we use later to trick the SASM debugger. In the current version (3.11.1), the debugger has a bug that causes that the registers are no longer updated in the register table, but end up as text in the output window.

With that, I can demonstrate an important feature of Intel CPUs or x86 compatible CPUs at the end of the chapter! But more on that later ...

Then we set the registers rax, rcx and rdx to 0 and the base register rbx to 10 as the starting value for the following loop.

Since we can only realize branches and loops with the help of jump commands, a label is used here, which we call _count_len_loop to describe the meaning of the label and to indicate that it is a loop.

With mov rax, rdx we load the result of the last run into rax. This is still 0 on the first run. Then we multiply rax by 10 (mul rbx). With mov dl, byte [input + rcx], we move a byte from the address of input in the dl register.

Since input is 20 bytes long, we have to explicitly specify with byte that we only want to load one byte. The [ ] tell the assembler that the second parameter is a memory address. The rcx is still 0 on the first pass but is then increased to 1 for the second pass, 2 for the third pass, etc.

With this, we load the start byte + 0, then the start byte + 1 - i.e. the second byte (index 1, if we see this as an array), etc., so this line ensures that we input byte by byte into go through the loop.

In order to understand the following comparisons and calculations, we should first take a look at the ASCII table. I provide you here the important parts:

Dez.	Hex.	Char	Dez.	Hex.	Char	Dez.	Hex.	Char	Dez.	Hex.	Char
48	0x30	0	49	0x31	1	50	0x32	2	51	0x33	3
52	0x34	4	53	0x35	5	54	0x36	6	55	0x37	7
56	0x38	8	57	0x39	9	58	0x3a	:	59	0x3b	;

You can see here that the number 0 has the value 48 or 0x30 in hexadecimal in the ASCII table.

So if the bit pattern of one of the bytes of the user input which we interpret as an integer is less than 48 (cmp dl, 48 and jb _errNan) or greater than 57 (cmp dl, 57 and ja _errNan), then the input cannot be any integer. So we jump to _errNan and issue an error message.

The rest of the loop deals with the conversion from the text representation of the number to the numerical value. If we now subtract from the byte value 48, we get the numerical value (sub rdx, 48). Compare that with the table - eg 50 – 48 = 2 - so the text "2" becomes the number 2!

Merging the number then does the add rdx, rax. To understand the process even better, I illustrate the process a little more precisely:

```
1 2 3                 mul bx              sub rdx, 48              add rdx, rax
| | |
| | |________> 12 x 10 = 120             51 - 48 = 3             3 + 120 = 123
| |__________>  1 x 10 =  10             50 - 48 = 2             2 +  10 =  12
|____________>  0 x 10 =   0             49 - 48 = 1             1 +   0 =   1
```

Here we have to read the illustration from bottom to top.

After adding rdx and rax together, we increase ecx by one (inc ecx) and then compare the next byte in input with 0xA (the line feed character). So after we have processed the first character, we compare whether there is a newline character in the second character, after processing the second character, whether the third character is a newline, etc.

If the comparison is not positive, we jump to the label _count_len_loop with jne. If the comparison is not correct, the code simply continues at this point and executes the next instruction.

If the first character were the newline character because the user made no entry and only pressed Enter, then the cmp dl, 48 and jb _errNan would ensure that an error is outputted. The registers have been deliberately set so that the current end result ends up in rdx in each run. The mul command in the second line of the loop code would empty any fragments of previous data anyway and so we save an additional xor rdx, rdx or mov rdx, 0 in the loop.

So there is a lot of tinkering in such a "simple" task as converting text "123" into the number 123.

Then we have something new again: push rdx puts the current numerical value on the so-called stack when leaving the loop. This is necessary because we will use rax, rcx and rdx in the next system call - of course, we would still have rbx free, but if we already use so many registers, in my opinion, it is clearer that we will store a value for later use on the stack as if we were playing desperately "Register Mikado" and pushing values around in circles.

In 64-bit processors, we have also the registers r8 - r15 but this habit or this programming style has set in my mind when I learned assembly in the 32-bit era. Apart from that, a system call could also overwrite rbx because it has to work with the same registers as the rest of the program!

You can imagine the stack as a storage basket on your desk - if you don't need a sheet of paper with notes, you can put it on top of the stack in the basket and then remove it later and continue to work with it. That should be enough at this point, we will do more with the stack in the next chapter.

Then follows a write syscall, in which we output the number. Since we start counting from 0, the counter is at 3 when we reach the fourth byte. In this case, that's just fine for us because we don't want to include the line break!

With pop rax we get the numerical value of the input back from the stack and place it in rax in order to then compare it with cmp rax, 10. jb _isDigit then jumps to the corresponding label if the entry corresponds to a digit. Otherwise, the code in _isNumber is executed.

In both cases, we jump over _errNan with jmp _end but we already know that from the last example.

In _end we complete the previously started write system call and end the program.

If you want to debug the whole program then please deactivate the syscall command in the read system call and activate call _fakeSyscall. Otherwise, the debugger will go crazy.

The call instruction is a special type of jump in which the program remembers where it was before the jump. The ret command (return) jumps from the function back to the position immediately after the function call. So, the program is continued with the instruction after the call command as soon as you exit the function with ret.

Within the function, we load the start address of the memory location input into the rax register. For repetition - in other assemblers, you should use lea rax, [input].

LITTLE ENDIAN AND BIG ENDIAN

The line `mov [rax], dword 0x0A333231` is interesting. `[rax]` means that we want to access the memory address that is in `rax` stored and not the `rax` register itself, `dword` indicates the size of the data to be moved. The `dword` stands for a 4 byte value.

The four possible sizes would be:

```
byte     8-bit   1 Byte
word    16-bit   2 Byte
dwort   32-bit   4 Byte (double-word)
qwort   64-bit   8 Byte (quad-word)
```

If we now separate the hexadecimal values after every byte we get: `0A 33 32 31`

If you compare this with the ASCII table, you get: `NEWLINE 3 2 1` - exactly the reverse order of the bytes. This byte order is called Little Endian. The opposite of this is called Big Endian and would be the order of bytes as we would expect `1 2 3 NEWLINE` or `0x3132330A` but since x86 processors work in the Little Endian system, we must pay attention to this when assigning multiple bytes in the same time!

It is also very important that it is the **byte order** and **not the bit order**! If you reverse the bit order, you will only get garbage data.

FUNCTION PARAMETERS, RETURN VALUES AND THE STACK

In most cases, functions require some input data to process. In other programming languages, parameters can be passed when functions are called. In assembler it is more like global variables - you put the data in the registers that the function uses later, just like in a system call.

The problem is that you often want to save the current status before calling a function. Under 32-bit assembly there was the `pusha` command to save all registers on the stack and `popa` to get all registers from the stack again - these two commands are no longer supported in the 64-bit assembly. Usually, you also do not need all registers and as you will see, these commands can be easily copied using macros.

It can also happen that you need want to save the flags - therefore exist the commands `pushf` and `popf` store and restore the flags.

Alternatively, you can also put the parameters on the stack. This must then happen in reverse order since the last value placed on the stack is the first to be taken down by the function.

But let's take a closer look at an example:

```
section .bss
    text    resb 100

section .text
    global      _start

    int_to_str:
        mov     rcx, 10
        push    0xA

        _div_loop:
            xor     rdx, rdx
            div     rcx
            add     rdx, 48
            push    rdx
            cmp     rax, 0
            jnz     _div_loop

        mov     rax, 0
```

```
_store_loop:
    pop       rdx
    mov       [rbx + rax], byte rdx
    inc       rax
    cmp       rdx, 0xA
    jne       _store_loop

    ret

_start:
    mov       rax, 1234
    mov       rbx, text
    call      int_to_str

    ; write-Syscall
    mov       rdx, rax           ; return val of function (string length)
    mov       rax, 1
    mov       rdi, 1
    mov       rsi, text
    syscall

    ; exit-Syscall
    mov       rax, 60
    mov       rdi, 0
    syscall
```

Here I use the `.bss` section again to reserve 100 bytes of memory at the address of the label `text`.

Then I first define the function in the `.text` section. It is not necessarily prescribed that way, but I have got used to it. But you can also do this after the `exit` syscall, the main thing is not to set the function in the middle of the main program. Although this would also be possible, it is very confusing.

In addition, for me, normal labels begin with a `_`, labels that initiate a function have no leading underscore. This is also not a requirement, just my attempt to differentiate between the labels.

Before we look at the function, let's have a look at the main program. Here we put a number (1234) in `rax` and the start address of `text` in `rbx`. Since I learned with 32-bit assembly I used always the order as for a Syscall (eax, ebx, ecx, edx) for passing the parameters. This is also completely irrelevant because there are no fixed rules here either.

The reason why I chose the number for the function call first is simply that I would need it in `rax` for the division anyway. It is quite normal in assembly that one or the other time you have to refactor the code again to use registers differently to avoid unnecessary `mov` instructions.

After the function call, the main program makes a `write` syscall and then ends.

After we have already seen how to convert a number into a number, let us consider the opposite way here.

First, we move the `10` into the `rcx` register (`mov  rcx,  10`) as a divisor. Then we put the newline character on the stack.

In the `_div_loop` we empty the `rdx` register with `xor rdx,  rdx` in order not to produce any calculation errors. As you will remember, `rdx:rax` are combined into a large 128-bit register when dividing and since the rest of the division ends up in `rdx`, we have to empty this register before each run. Since we do not know whether `rdx` was used before the function call and contains data or not, we do the `xor  rdx,  rdx` as the first operation and not as the last before the jump.

Then we divide `rax` by `rcx` - the result ends up in `rax` and the rest in `rdx`. Then the number 48 is added to `rdx` to make the corresponding text from a number. So here we work with the ASCII table again.

`push  rdx` places the character created in this way on the stack and `cmp  rax,  0` compares whether there are any more digits left in `rax` - if so, we jump to the beginning of the loop with `jnz _div_loop`.

I illustrate the process again:

```
1234 / 10 =        123 (rax)      4 rest (rdx) + 48     =>    "4"
 123 / 10 =         12 (rax)      3 rest (rdx) + 48     =>    "3"
  12 / 10 =          1 (rax)      2 rest (rdx) + 48     =>    "2"
   1 / 10 =          0 (rax)      1 rest (rdx) + 48     =>    "1"
```

The reason why I put it on the stack is that we get the numbers in reverse order, so the stack is perfect in that case to reverse them back to the right order.

After the first loop, the character "1" is at the top of the stack, the character "2" is at the second position, etc. So we only need to pick text from the stack character by character until we get the newline character that we put the stack first. This is exactly what `_store_loop` does!

Take a character (`pop  rdx`), place the character in the appropriate place in the storage space (`mov [rbx + rax],  byte rdx`), increase `rax` (`inc  rax`), compare whether the current character is the newline character (`cmp rdx,  0xA`) and if not repeat the loop (`jne _store_loop`).

The reason why I used `rax` to count this time is that I want to provide the string length as a return parameter. Normally I would use the registers according to their original use to make the program easier to understand and therefore use `rcx` as a "counter variable", but this is not mandatory either, just a good coding practice. Then I would have the return value in `rcx`. You can postpone this with a `mov` but sometimes you just have to break the "rules" in assembly.

The return value is also important at this point because we need a length calculation of the string for the `write` syscall.

Again, I try to stick to the way the syscalls work, and I use `rax` as a return parameter in all of my functions. Alternatively, you could also put the parameters on the stack. This would then have to be in the reverse order in which they are expected in the main program.

MACROS AND CODE LIBRARIES

The syntax of how macros are defined depends on the assembler. What I'm showing you here is specific to NASM and works differently in other assemblers! In theory, it is even possible that a very rudimentary assembler does not offer this function at all. As far as I know, there are also macros in FASM and MASM.

It makes sense to set up code libraries for macros. After all, the purpose of macros is to make frequently used program parts accessible using a shorthand notation. Since you could most likely need these in several projects, you can write macros and functions in a separate file. I named the file for this example my_lib.inc - let's look at the content:

```
%macro endprg 1
    mov        rax, 60
    mov        rdi, %1
    syscall
%endmacro
```

A macro is defined between `%macro` and `%endmacro`. `%macro` is followed by the name under which the macro is called later - here it would be `endprg`. 1 indicates that the macro is expecting an argument. A macro can expect no (0) or more arguments.

We can write any assembler code in the macro itself. The line `mov rdi,%1` is striking in this example. This assigns the first argument which is passed when the macro is called to the `rdi` register. If you remember, this is the status code with which the program is ended.

You can also see some potential problems with this example. The macro works with the same registers as the rest of the code - you won't find anything like local function variables in assembly! No matter whether you call syscalls, macros or functions - everything works with the same registers as the main program.

It is therefore up to us to communicate which registers are used so that everyone who uses the macro can save data that may be required later on the stack or move it to another register. This is not a problem at the end of the program, but in the next example, it will be a problem!

Now let's take a look at the "Hello world" example of how it looks with our new macro:

```
%include "my_lib.inc"

section .data
    text        db "Hello World!", 0xA
    len         equ $-text

section .text
    global      _start

    _start:
        mov         rax, 1
        mov         rdi, 1
        mov         rsi, text
        mov         rdx, len
        syscall

        endprg      0
```

I highlighted the changes in bold. First, we import the library file with `%include "my_lib.inc"` and then we can call the macro with `endprg 0`. Here the 0 ends up in the macro in `%1` and then in `rdi`.

If a macro expects more than one argument, the arguments can be separated by a comma (`,`) as usual with other assembly commands.

Let's define another macro in our `my_lib.inc`:

```
%macro sleep 1
    mov rcx, %1
    _wait_loop:
        nop
        dec rcx
        jnz _wait_loop
%endmacro
```

The macro `sleep` again expects 1 argument, which is placed in `rcx`. Then the label `_wait_loop` follows. In the loop body we find `nop`, `dec rcx` and the `jnz` command. So we do nothing (nop), decrement `rcx` and if `rcx` has not yet reached 0, we repeat the code again. Basically, the `nop` instruction would not be necessary since `dec` also occupies one CPU cycle, but we then "dawdle" two CPU cycles in the loop body.

Here is the danger that I mentioned earlier clearly visible - if we have data in `rcx` that we still need after calling `sleep`, we have to save it somewhere else otherwise our program would continue to work with the value 0 in `rcx` after `sleep` and most likely not deliver the desired result or even crash!

Then we use this macro in our "Hello world" example:

```
%include "my_lib.inc"

section .data
    text        db "Hello World!", 0xA
    len         equ $-text

section .text
    global      _start

    _start:
        sleep       100
        mov         rax, 1
        mov         rdi, 1
        mov         rsi, text
        mov         rdx, len
        syscall

        sleep       200
        endprg      0
```

Here I have included `sleep` twice in the code to show you another problem. When translating, the code of the macro is simply copied to the place where we call it. This now means that we have twice the `_wait_loop` label in the code.

Since this is not allowed, NASM tells us this with the following error: `/tmp/SASM/program.asm:18: error: symbol `_wait_loop ' redefined`. Of course, labels have to be unique, because otherwise, the assembler wouldn't know which to which label he has to jump when a command will tell him to do so.

Of course, the developers of NASM have considered this and provided a solution to such problems. To do this, we need to adjust the macro as follows:

```
%macro sleep 1
    mov rcx, %1
    %%_wait_loop:
        nop
        dec rcx
        jnz %%_wait_loop
%endmacro
```

The specification of `%%` in front of the label ensures that a unique ID is used for every call - if we examine the finished program with a disassembler and debugger such as `radare2 / Cutter` or `IDA64`, we will see that the labels are now called `..@3._wait_loop` and `..@4._wait_loop`.

To debug a program using `radare2` or `IDA64`, you must first convert it to an executable and then load that executable into `IDA64` or `Cutter`. The assembly code is calculated back on the basis of the opcodes found in the file. Therefore, the code is not always exactly the one you wrote. This can be due to optimizations when creating the code or the disassembler displays an alternative mnemonic. Especially with jump instructions, it often happens that completely different spellings than those you use appear - this is because different jump instructions are converted to the same opcode.

In addition, you can disassemble everything in these programs - such as the strings, etc. This may provide a completely pointless assembly code - it is up to you to decide what should be treated within the file and how.

You can also define constants with `equ` in libraries in order to use them in your programs and make them even easier to understand - for example:

```
LF  equ 0xA
NUL equ 0x0
```

You could then use this when creating strings:

```
text db "Hello World!", LF
```

As indicated in the previous chapter, I would like to show you my `push_all` and `pop_all` macros:

```nasm
%macro push_all 0
    push rax
    push rbx
    push rcx
    push rdx
%endmacro

%macro pop_all 0
    pop rdx
    pop rcx
    pop rbx
    pop rax
%endmacro
```

Since I primarily work with the registers `rax`, `rbx`, `rcx` and `rdx`, I only considered those registers in my `push_all` variant. If you want to test these macros here would be a small test code:

```nasm
section .data
    text        db "Hello World!", LINEFEED
    len         equ $-text

section .text
    global      _start

    _start:
        mov         rax, 1
        mov         rbx, 2
        mov         rcx, 3
        mov         rdx, 4
        push_all

        mov         rax, 1
        mov         rdi, 1
        mov         rsi, text
        mov         rdx, len
        syscall

        pop_all
        inc         rdx

        endprg      0
```

The SASM debugger has its difficulties here too, which is why you could switch to Cutter + radare2. You can find these tools at: https://rada.re/n/

Another very good debugger is IDA64 which you can download for free (for private and non-commercial use) at https://www.hex-rays.com/products/ida/support/download_freeware/.

CLI ARGUMENTS

Commandline arguments are inputs for the program that the user passes directly when calling the program. That would be, for example, the path that can be passed to `ls` or the source and target file or target folder for the `mv` or `cp` command in Linux.

At the same time, this is the simplest form of user interaction for us developers - we do not need to query user input and we still receive inputs. For users, CLI Arguments (command-line interface) have the advantage that they can be used in scripts and that could, for example, allow automate the work with the program.

In Linux the given arguments are automatically put on the stack when the program is started - all we have to do is read the arguments from the stack.

As a small project to illustrate this, I have considered a very simple encryption tool for this the next chapter:

```
%include "my_lib.inc"

section .data
    usage       db 0xA,"Usage:",0xA,"-------",0xA, "xorcrypt [password]
                    [filename]",0xA,0xA
    lenUsage    equ $-usage

    passErr     db 0xA,"Password-Error: Min. length is 8 characters!",0xA,0xA
    lenErr      equ $-passErr

section .bss
    fileCont    resb 2048

section .text
    global      _start

    _start:
        pop     rcx                         ; argc

        ; check length of argc
        cmp     rcx, 3
        jne     _print_usage_and_exit
```

```nasm
; pop args from stack
pop     rax                             ; path
pop     rbx                             ; arg1
pop     r9                              ; arg2

; read password into register
mov     rcx, 0
_load_byte_loop:
    shl     r8, 8
    mov     r8b, byte [rbx + rcx]
    inc     rcx
    cmp     [rbx + rcx], byte 0x0
    jne     _load_byte_loop

cmp     rcx, 8
jb              _print_pw_error_and_exit

; read file
; xor data
; write file

 endprg  0

_print_usage_and_exit:
    mov     rax, 1
    mov     rdi, 1
    mov     rsi, usage
    mov     rdx, lenUsage
    syscall

    endprg  1

_print_pw_error_and_exit:
    mov     rax, 1
    mov     rdi, 1
    mov     rsi, passErr
    mov     rdx, lenErr
    syscall

    endprg  2
```

I don't need to explain the `.data` and `.bss` section anymore ...

In the main program, we read the number of arguments passed (`argc`) into the `rcx` register. I should mention that at least one argument is always passed, and that is the path to the called file (`path`).

Then we use `cmp rcx, 3` to check if we have received 3 arguments. Compare the usage string that specifies `xorcrypt [password] [filename]` (path, arg1 and arg2). If this comparison fails, we jump to label `_print_usage_and_exit` with `jne` and output the usage message in this label. Please also note the `endprg 1`, with which we define that the program was ended with error no. 1.

When started in the terminal, this exit code is saved in `$?` and can then be used, for example, to react to errors in bash scripts. In addition, the logical combinations of shell commands (&& and ||) also evaluate this exit code.

Then we get the pointer to the path string in `rax`, the pointer to `arg1` in `rbx` and the pointer to `arg2` in `r9`. Just like `path`, all arguments are null-terminated strings. These are character strings with a NULL byte (`0x0`) marking the end.

In order to encrypt the data with the bit pattern of the password, we have to put it into a register. For this, we first set the counter register back to 0 (`mov rcx, 0`) and then define the label `_load_byte_loop`.

At the beginning of each loop-run, we shift the bit pattern with `shl r8, 8` to the left by 8 bits (1 byte) to make room for the next character.

Moving a byte into `r8b` (the bottom 8 bits of `r8`). You already know the addressing scheme base address + counter. Since we constantly need the bit pattern of the password, I will use `r8` for this so that we do not have to keep storing data on the stack and getting it back over and over again.

Then we increase the counter (`inc rcx`) and check whether the next byte is the NUL character (`cmp [rbx + rcx], byte 0x0`). If the end of the string has not yet been reached, we jump to `_load_byte_loop` with `jne`.

Attentive readers will have noticed that I lose the front bytes if the password is longer than 8 characters because more does not fit in a 64-bit register. That's right, you could use a variety of registers to hold more bytes and use them later combined, but this was too much code for the example in this book. So far you have learned enough to do this yourself as an exercise if you want to.

XOR is not the very best method to encrypt data anyway, but we don't want to develop groundbreaking new high-end encryption here, but learn how to use CLI-arguments and files.

After leaving this loop again, we check whether the password length is 8 bytes or more (`cmp  rcx, 8`) and if not, we jump with `jb _print_pw_error_and_exit` to output the corresponding error message after which we end the program with the error code 2.

Before the `endprg 0` there are three comments to remind me what is still missing. In addition, in the next chapter in which we will finish the program, I will only publish this code in order not to fill several pages with code that we already know.

In this sense, the comments also serve as a guide for you.

WORKING WITH FILES

Here we use Syscalls again. I would like to briefly break down the open syscall and show you how and where you can find the necessary information …

I want to remind you the file unistd_64.h which you may find under /usr/src/linux-headers-5.3.0-53-generic/arch/x86/include/generated/uapi/asm/unistd_64.h. In this file are the ID-numbers of the Syscalls defined. We will use the following in this chapter:

```
#define __NR_read 0
#define __NR_write 1
#define __NR_open 2
#define __NR_close 3
```

If we run man 2 open in the terminal, we get the following manpage:

```
OPEN(2)                       Linux Programmer's Manual                       OPEN(2)

NAME
       open, openat, creat - open and possibly create a file

SYNOPSIS
       #include <sys/types.h>
       #include <sys/stat.h>
       #include <fcntl.h>

       int open(const char *pathname, int flags);
       int open(const char *pathname, int flags, mode_t mode);
```

We need three parameters: a pointer to the string pathname, flags and mode.

When we scroll further down in the manpage we found a pretty deep explanation of the mode parameter:

```
S_IRWXU  00700 user (file owner) has read, write, and execute permission
S_IRUSR  00400 user has read permission
S_IWUSR  00200 user has write permission
S_IXUSR  00100 user has execute permission
... etc.
```

The parameter mode is nothing else than the numerical representation of the file permissions - e.g.:

`0644` for `-rw-r--r--` or
`0750` for `-rwxr-x---` etc.

However, what we don't find is an explanation of the values for flags. Let's look at the manpage, then we see three include statements at the top under SYNOPSIS. Logically, the constants used should have been defined somewhere in one of these three files.

I searched in all these files for that constants and quickly show you where I found it. Executing `locate fcntl.h` in the Linux terminal provides the following list:

```
/usr/src/linux-headers-5.3.0-53/arch/alpha/include/uapi/asm/fcntl.h
/usr/src/linux-headers-5.3.0-53/arch/arm/include/uapi/asm/fcntl.h
/usr/src/linux-headers-5.3.0-53/arch/arm64/include/uapi/asm/fcntl.h
/usr/src/linux-headers-5.3.0-53/arch/ia64/include/uapi/asm/fcntl.h
/usr/src/linux-headers-5.3.0-53/arch/m68k/include/uapi/asm/fcntl.h
/usr/src/linux-headers-5.3.0-53/arch/mips/include/uapi/asm/fcntl.h
/usr/src/linux-headers-5.3.0-53/arch/parisc/include/uapi/asm/fcntl.h
/usr/src/linux-headers-5.3.0-53/arch/powerpc/include/uapi/asm/fcntl.h
/usr/src/linux-headers-5.3.0-53/arch/sparc/include/uapi/asm/fcntl.h
/usr/src/linux-headers-5.3.0-53/arch/x86/include/uapi/asm/fcntl.h
/usr/src/linux-headers-5.3.0-53/include/linux/fcntl.h
/usr/src/linux-headers-5.3.0-53/include/uapi/asm-generic/fcntl.h
/usr/src/linux-headers-5.3.0-53/include/uapi/linux/fcntl.h
```

Since we are writing x86 code, I first looked at the file `/usr/src/linux-headers-5.3.0-53/arch/x86/include/uapi/asm/fcntl.h`, but it only contained the following line:

```
#include <asm-generic/fcntl.h>
```

So i opened `/usr/src/linux-headers-5.3.0-53/include/uapi/asm-generic/fcntl.h` and found the following lines:

```
#define O_RDONLY        00000000
#define O_WRONLY        00000001
#define O_RDWR          00000002
...etc.
```

After that I added the following constants in the `.data` segment:

```
O_RDONLY      equ 0
O_WRONLY      equ 1
O_RDWR        equ 2
O_CREAT       equ 64
```

We can now use these named constants and do not have to remember the numbers. Such things can also be done in libraries and they make your code more readable.

I only use capital letters for constant names to distinguish them from labels. This is also not mandatory but provides more clarity in the code. I also chose the names of the constants exactly as in the header file or exactly as in the manpage.

This habit means that I don't always have to look around in my library-code to find out how I named something.

READ FILES

Armed with this knowledge, we can now complete the program from the last chapter. First, we have to read the file:

```
; read file
mov     rax, 2
mov     rdi, r9
mov     rsi, O_RDONLY
mov     rdx, 644o
syscall                         ; open-Syscall -> file-descriptor in rax

mov     rdi, rax                ; fd from syscall before
mov     rax, 0
mov     rsi, fileCont
mov     rdx, 2048
syscall                         ; read-Syscall

; store length on stack
push    rax

; calculate how much qwords of data to process
xor     rdx, rdx
mov     rcx, 8
div     rcx
push    rax

; close-Syscall
mov     rax, 3                  ; no mov rsi, ... needed
syscall                         ; rsi still hold fd
```

This is done with three syscalls - open, read and close! We hand over for the open-syscall the Syscall-ID in rax (2), the pointer to the file name in rdi, the previously defined constant O_RDONLY or 0 in rsi and the mode. The mode would be 644 as an octal number - therefore we write 644o and mark the value with the o in the end as octal.

When opening a file, the mode does not really mater. Here you could also simply enter 0 or not use the register at all. However, I have got used to always specifying this as 644. To ensure that any other data in the rdx register is overwritten and does not cause any problems and further to indicate what this register stands for.

The open syscall returns us a file descriptor (fd) which we will move to rdi for the read syscall.

In this case, we read 2048 bytes in the memory area with the label fileCont. This is not ideal! As long as the file is smaller than 2048 bytes, we read the entire file, but as soon as the file is larger, we only read the first 2048 bytes of the file!

To solve this, you can increase the reserved space, but eventually, it becomes impractical. After all, your program shouldn't request 100GB RAM and even that might not be enough if someone wants to encrypt a virtual hard drive or gigantic databases, for example.

One solution is to edit the file bit by bit and to use several read syscalls in a loop. Of course, you would have to open an output file and encrypt and write the data before the next read syscall. At this point, I leave that to you as a small exercise ...

If you don't get a positive value from a syscall in rax, that's an error code. You can find these codes defined in the files /usr/src/linux-headers-5.3.0-53/include/uapi/asm-generic/errno.h and /usr/src/linux-headers-5.3.0-53/include/ uapi / asm-generic / errno-base.h:

```
#define       EPERM        1      /* Operation not permitted */
#define       ENOENT       2      /* No such file or directory */
#define       ESRCH        3      /* No such process */
#define       EINTR        4      /* Interrupted system call */
#define       EIO          5      /* I/O error */
#define       ENXIO        6      /* No such device or address */
#define       E2BIG        7      /* Argument list too long */
#define       ENOEXEC      8      /* Exec format error */
#define       EBADF        9      /* Bad file number */
#define       ECHILD      10      /* No child processes */
#define       EAGAIN      11      /* Try again */
#define       ENOMEM      12      /* Out of memory */
#define       EACCES      13      /* Permission denied */
#define       EFAULT      14      /* Bad address */
... etc.
```

During development, I accidentally assigned an incorrect register to open-Syscall and then received error -14 (EFAULT). After a quick look at this file, I already knew where to look.

Since the close-syscall overwrites rax, rbx and rdx, we first have to get the number bytes read on the stack with push rax for later use.

Then we clean `rdx` with `xor rdx, rdx` to not to get any wrong results when dividing and put 8 in `rcx` (because the div operator does not allow a number as parameter, but only a register). Then we can calculate how many 64-bit or 8-byte blocks we have for encryption (`div rcx`) and save the result on the stack again (`push rax`).

In this case, we only save the number of whole blocks. The rest of the division in `rdx` is ignored and not encrypted either. I just left that out for space reasons. As an exercise, you are welcome to empty a register and in a second loop insert the remaining bytes individually as we did with the password, XOR and then individually push the bytes back into memory. I wanted to keep the example as short as possible here.

Alternatively, you can simply set the memory to a larger value, such as 200MB, and tell the user that this is the maximum file size. To do this, set the value for `fileCont` slightly larger than the desired maximum file size and check whether there is a smaller number of read bytes as the maximum size of the storage space after the `read` Syscall in `rax`.

Increase `resb`, `cmp` and depending on that eventually issue an error message if necessary...

WRITE FILES

Before we write the file, we must first encrypt the data in `fileCont`. If you are wondering how to decrypt the encrypted data again, this code demonstrates how XOR encryption works:

```
mov     rax, 0xAAAAAAAAAAAAAAAA    ; rax => 0xAAAAAAAAAAAAAAAA
mov     rbx, 0xBBBBBBBBBBBBBBBB    ; rax => 0xAAAAAAAAAAAAAAAA
xor     rax, rbx                   ; rax => 0x1111111111111111
xor     rax, rbx                   ; rax => 0xAAAAAAAAAAAAAAAA
```

If you apply a `xor` to data to encrypt it, you only have to `xor` the data one more time with the same pattern to get the original data back. So the double `xor`-encryption is about as secure as a software download from a russian warez-sites. After that is clear, let's look at how we encrypt the data:

```
        ; setup registers for loop
        pop     rcx
        mov     rbx, fileCont

        ; xor data
        _xor_file_loop:
            mov     rax, qword [rbx]
            xor     rax, r8
            mov     [rbx], rax

            add     rbx, 8
            dec     rcx
            jnz     _xor_file_loop

        ; write file
        mov     rax, 2
        mov     rdi, r9
        mov     rsi, O_WRONLY
        mov     rdx, 644o
        syscall                     ; open-Syscall

        mov     rdi, rax            ; fd from syscall before
        mov     rax, 1
        mov     rsi, fileCont
        pop     rdx                 ; get stored length from stack
        syscall                     ; write-Syscall
```

```
; close-Syscall
mov     rax, 3                          ; no mov rsi, ... needed
syscall                                 ; rsi still hold fd
```

First, we get the number of 8-byte blocks from the stack in `rcx` (pop rcx) and then we load the memory address from `fileCont` into `rbx` (mov rbx, fileCont)

Then follows the label `_xor_file_loop`, in which all encryption takes place. With `mov rax, qword [rbx]` we load a quad word (8 bytes of data) from the memory address in `rbx` to `rax`. Then we perform the `xor` operation with `r8` (the password or the last 8 bytes of the password) and write the data back to its storage location. This time we do not have to specify the size because the register `rax` specifies the size - only if we load data from a memory area into a register would we have to specify the operation size.

Then we add 8 to the memory address (add rbx, 8) to point to the start byte of the next 8-byte block and decrease the counter by one (dec rcx). If the counter has not yet reached 0, we jump to the beginning of the loop (jnz _xor_file_loop).

Then follows the `open` syscall with which we now open the file for writing (O_WRONLY). If we wanted to create a new file, we would have to specify the flag O_CREAT or the numeric value 64. Then a new file would be created with the rights specified in mode (rdx).

This is followed by the `write` Syscall, whereby we use `pop rdx` to reload the number of bytes read previously from the stack and use it for writing. Of course, it only makes sense to write as many bytes as we read before ...

Then the file is closed with the `close` Syscall.

FLOATING-POINT NUMBERS IN ASSEMBLY

Floating-point numbers (floats) are handled with their registers (eg `fpu0 - fpu7`) and their own set of commands or opcodes. In this chapter, I want to show you how to work with floats because it differs from the integers.

We also differentiate between "Single precision" with 32-bit and "Double precision" with 64-bit. Internally, the floating-point registers even work with 80-bit, which leads us too much into the details at this point. Therefore, I refer interested parties to the Intel Developer Manual.

Let's take a closer look at the structure of the 32- and 64-bit floating-point numbers:

32-bit:

1bit Sign	8-bit Exponent	23-bit Base-number

64-bit:

1bit Sign	11-bit Exponent	52-bit Base-number

As some readers already think, it looks suspiciously like the scientific spelling and basically, it is exactly that!

The peculiarity of the registers `fpu0 - fpu7` is that they work like the stack. Under 32-bit these registers were called `st0 - st7`. You should know that for example, IDA64 and `edb` still show the 32-bit names in the register overview.

In this project, however, I had the problem that I had accidentally saved the database in IDA64 and then no longer load a later, newly translated version of the code, since IDA always loaded and loaded the previously disassembled version from the database. Reloading the file with `File -> Load file -> Reload input file` was canceled with an error.

For this reason, I went the pragmatic way and since `Cutter` does not display the FPU registers, I switched to `edb`. The tool can be installed on many distributions with the package name `edb-debugger` or you can get the current version from Github:

https://github.com/eteran/edb-debugger

That is the code which we will analyze with the debugger:

```nasm
section .data
    list    dd  1.5
            dd  2.2
            dd  3.1
            dd -1.1
    lenList equ ($-list) / 4

section .text
    global      _start

    _start:
        mov     rcx, lenList
        mov     rbx, list

        finit
        fld     dword [rbx]
        dec     rcx

        _foreach_loop:
            add     rbx, 4
            fld     dword [rbx]
            fadd
            loop    _foreach_loop

        ; get result in stack and then in rax
        fstp    qword [rsp]
        pop     rax

        ; exit
        mov     rdi, 0
        mov     rax, 60
        syscall
```

On this occasion, I can also show you how to work with lists or arrays in assembly. In the `.data` section, we create the label `list`, under which we create four floating-point numbers, each with 32-bit.

dd stands for Define Double in the sense of Double Word and not double-precision! A double precision value with 64-bit would be created via dq (Define Quad)! In that case you would also have to work with equ ($ -list) / 8, qword [rbx] and add rbx, 8!

The commands `mov rcx, lenList` and `mov rbx, list` set the number of elements in `rcx` and the memory address of the list in `rbx`. Then comes the first new floating-point command.

`finit` (Floating point unit initialize) clears the FPU registers. `fld dword [rbx]` (Floating point Load) loads the first number into register 0 - the debugger should now show you `ST0 valid 1.5`. You will soon understand why this is so. Now that we have already loaded the first number, we have to decrease `rcx` by one (`dec rcx`).

Then follows our loop with the label `_foreach_loop` in which we add up the numbers. First, we add 4 to `rbx` to point to the second entry in the array (`list`). So you see arrays are nothing more than a series of values that are in the memory one behind the other and are addressed with an offset.

The `fld dword [rbx]` loads the second value into the FPU registers and `edb` now shows the following:

```
ST0     valid  2.20000004768371582031
ST1     valid  1.5
```

You will notice that the second value is incorrect and that we have minimal inaccuracy. You will understand why this is the case if we decode the result again by hand. After the example, you are welcome to rewrite the program with double precision and examine it again. Then you will understand why 64-bit float numbers are called double precision!

As you can see, `fadd` doesn't take any parameters - that's why we have to put the two values on the stack. As soon as we execute the command, we see:

```
ST7     empty  2.20000004768371582031  (displayed in gray)
ST0     valid  3.70000004768371582031
```

You can understand `fadd` as `st0 = st0 + st1`! In this case, `st1` will also be emptied immediately and we will no longer consider the display of the old value in `st7` in the future. The `loop` command is also new in this example and replaces three commands:

```
dec     rcx
cmp     rcx, 0
jnz     _foreach_loop
```

So there are a few more commands than the basic commands we've covered in the book till now. Therefore, you should also take a look at the Developer Manual! In this book, I wanted to introduce you to programming with assembly and not to create a complete command reference ...

At the next loop pass we see after `fld`:

```
ST0    valid  3.09999990463256835938
ST1    valid  3.70000004768371582031
```

and after the addition we see:

```
ST0    valid  6.79999990463256835938
```

After the last addition we get:

```
ST0    valid  5.69999992847442626953
```

The `fstp qword [rsp]` is not a mistake - we worked with single-precision all the time, but now we want to put a double-precision value from the FPU register into the stack. This makes sense that the entire register is overwritten and any existing bytes in `rax` that would not be overwritten with a 32-bit value do not falsify the result!

The floating-point unit (FPU) does this conversion for us automatically and places the 8 bytes on the stack which we then load into the accumulator register with `pop rax`.

With that, our program is almost done - we will now use Python to convert the bit pattern in `rax` into a number since this is relatively complex! You could also link the file `/lib64/ld-linux-x86-64.so.2` to your code and then call the `printf` function from assembly! But I leave that to you as an exercise!

We should now have `0x4016ccccc8000000` in `rax`. With a double click on the register in edb you get a window in which you can also copy or change the number.

Let's first convert the hexadecimal number to the bit pattern using Python:

```
>>> print(bin(int("0x4016ccccc8000000", 16)))
0b100000000001011011001100110011001100100000000000000000000000000000
```

I split that pattern up into individual bytes so that we can read it easier:

01000000 00010110 11001100 11001100 11001000 00000000 00000000 00000000

Python cuts any leading zeros so you need to pay attention and add missing digits! I have already added the missing zero for the positive sign above and mark it in bold!

Then we can split the bit-pattern up in the parts for a 32-bit float:

1-bit Sign	11-bit Exponent	52-bit Base-number
0	10000000001	0110110011001100110011001001000000000000000000000000000000000

The 0 stands for a positive number and a 1 would indicate a negative number.

With the exponent we have to do the following calculation:

```
>>> print(int("10000000001", 2) - int("01111111111", 2))
2
```

This is because we only "think" the leading 1 in the base number and therefore we have basically 53- instead of the 52bit. The calculation is always an exponent bit pattern minus 0b01111111111!

The remaining bits of the base-number are to be understood as follows:

```
   0     1     1     0     1     1     0     0     1     1     ...
1 + 0/2 + 1/4 + 1/8 + 0/16 + 1/32 + 1/64 + 0/128 + 0/256 + 1/512 + 1/1024 ...
```

As I said, we only think of the leading 1. In this case, the individual bits stand for fractions based on 2. Therefore, for example, 1.5 (1 + 1/2) or 1.125 (1 + 1/8) or 2.75 (1 + 1/2 + 1/4) can be represented without rounding errors, but many other numbers are only an approximation!

Therefore, you should never check for equality with floating-point numbers, but check whether the difference is below a certain limit!

You can see the floating-point number problem in Python, for example, using this statement:

```
>>> (0.1 * 3) == 0.3
False
```

So three times 0.1 is not equal to 0.3 for the PC! As an exercise in assembly, you are welcome to investigate why this is so ...

Now let's calculate the base number:

```
>>> 1 + 0/2 + 1/4 + 1/8 + 0/16 + 1/32 + 1/64 + 0/128 + 0/256 + 1/512 + 1/1024
1.4248046875
```

So we have $1.4248046875e2$ as a result. Since we work in binary, the e2 is to be understood as 2^2 and not 10^2! So we calculate that:

```
>>> 1.4248046875 * (2 ** 2)
5.69921875
```

If we had taken the other digits of the binary chain into account, the result would be much more precise! The more "decimal places" we have, the smaller the calculation error and the better the precision!

You have the `fsub`, `fdiv` and `fmul` command families for the other basic arithmetic operations with floats. Take a look at the corresponding documentation and practice until you really understand how it works.

AFTERWORD

I hope I was able to bring you closer to assembly and show you that assembly is not that difficult! Programming with it takes getting used to and requires discipline and good documentation to find your way around easily, but once you get used to doing everything by hand and getting by with the few registers, assembly programming then quite easily.

Use the sample programs and experiment with them and debug preferably every example until you fully understand what's going on. In my opinion, this is the best way to learn.

Have fun and keep practising!

Mark B.

FEEDBACK & CRITICISM

If you want to get rid of criticism, suggestions or even just have questions, please send me an email to `mark.b@post.cz`.

I will try to realize your input in further book projects and new editions.

BOOK RECOMMENDATIONS

19,95 USD

ISBN: 978-1703311327

Many interested people are tingling with the topic of hacking and this book shows you how to test your knowledge completely legally in practice and earn even good money.The usual way to do such a thing would be to be involved as a Pentester only that would require normally expensive certifications or at least verifiable experience in the area! That's where Bug Bounty programs come in. As a rule, everyone is welcome here, from beginners to experienced Pentesters. Besides, no specific certifications, training or something else is required. That's what allows beginners to apply their skills in real-life examples, to earn their "first spurs" and to gain verifiable experience as Pentester.Follow us on the first steps to be a Pentester and learn how to test for the vulnerabilities to specific attacks and what tools can be used to achieve that. We also show you how to write good reports and which strategy has served us the best in real tests. This book makes you fit to get started in this job. Here we reveal common misconceptions of developers and less obvious attacks with which you score in practice.

5,99 USD

ISBN: 978-3746093475

YAML is a proven data serialization language that has been on the market since 2001. There are also parsers for pretty much all common programming languages.In addition, the overhead is significantly lower than with XML and especially the predefined tags make YAML a bit more flexible because you can define the data type according to the data which makes subsequent testing and conversion of the parsed data unnecessary.

That's why YAML is sometimes better than XML or JSON. In addition, YAML is used by many programs for data storage or configuration files.Still, I YAML very easy to learn and master. We invite you to take a look at this interesting language and to learn how to handle YAML data in Python and PHP ...

Python is an easy to learn, yet very diverse and powerful programming language and that for the language of choice for many hackers.

Learn to write your own tools and use them on Kali Linux to see how hackers attack systems and exploit vulnerabilities. Developing your own tools will give you a much deeper understanding of how and why attacks work. After a short introduction to programming with Python, you will learn to write a wide variety of hacking tools using many practical examples.

By integrating existing tools such as Metasploit and Nmap, scripts become even more efficient and shorter. Use the knowledge you have gained here to test your systems for security holes and close them before others can take advantage of them!

19,99 EUR

ISBN: 978-3752686159

OpenSCAD is not like other CAD solutions and that is exactly what makes it so flexible and easy to learn.

With this book, you will learn how easy it is to develop your own models from scratch in OpenSCAD and then export them for 3D printing or other manufacturing processes. Besides, I'll show you how you can import and process 2D and 3D models from other CAD programs...

I will also show you how I approach a design and why I choose a solution for a specific situation. This gives you a practical insight into working with OpenSCAD!

14,99 EUR

ISBN: 978-3752685602